New American STREAMLINE

BERNARD HARTLEY & PETER VINEY

CONNECTIONS

New American STREAMLINE

BERNARD HARTLEY & PETER VINEY

CONNECTIONS

An intensive American English series for intermediate students
Student Book

REVISED BY PETER VINEY

With contributions by BERNARD HARTLEY

Oxford University Press

Oxford University Press

198 Madison Avenue
New York, NY 10016 USA

Great Clarendon Street
Oxford OX2 6DP England

Oxford New York
Athens Auckland Bangkok Bogotá Buenos Aires
Cape Town Chennai Dar es Salaam
Delhi Florence Hong Kong Istanbul Karachi Kolkata
Kuala Lumpur Madrid Melbourne Mexico City
Mumbai Nairobi Paris São Paulo Shanghai
Singapore Taipei Tokyo Toronto Warsaw

and associated companies in
Berlin Ibadan

OXFORD is a trademark of Oxford University Press

Copyright © 1995 B. Hartley, P. Viney, and Oxford
University Press

Library of Congress Cataloging-in-Publication Data

Hartley, Bernard.
    Connections: an intensive American English series
for intermediate students: student book / Bernard
Hartley & Peter Viney.
        p.   cm. — (New American Streamline)
    "Based on the American adaptation by Flamm/
Northam Authors and Publishers Services, Inc."
    Includes index.
    ISBN 0-19-434829-6 (student bk.). — ISBN 0-19-
434831-8 (teacher bk.). — ISBN 0-19-434832-6 (cassette).
— ISBN 0-19-434848-2 (CD)
    1. English language—Textbooks for foreign speak-
ers. 2. English language—United States. 3.
Americanisms. I. Viney, Peter. II. Title. III. Series:
Hartley, Bernard. New American Streamline.
PE1128.H3755   1994
428.3'4—dc20   94-7788

Printing (last digit) 10 9 8 7

Printed in Hong Kong

Based on the American adaptation by Flamm/Northam
Authors and Publishers Services, Inc.

Editorial Manager: Susan Lanzano
Editor: Ken Mencz
Designer: Sharon Hudak
Art Buyer: Stevie Pettus-Famulari
Picture Researcher: Paul Hahn
Production Manager: Abram Hall

Cover illustration by: Pete Kelly

Illustrations and realia by: Ray Alma, Dolores Bego,
Douglas Buchman, Chris Costello, John Edens, Kelly
Hume, Valerie Marsella, Paddy Mounter, Joe Peery, Tom
Powers, Tim Raglin, David Slonim, Anne Stanley, Darren
Thompson, Stephan Van Litsenborg, Rose Zgodzinski

Photography by: Peter Chin; Richard Haynes, Cynthia
Hill, Dennis Kitchen, Stephen Ogilvy
(If notified, the publisher will be pleased to rectify any
errors or omissions at the earliest opportunity.)

*The publisher would like to thank the following for their
permission to reproduce photographs:* Allsport;
Camerique/H. Armstrong Roberts; © Chad Ehlers/
International Stock; Blas Elias courtesy of Ludwig
Drums, a division of The Selmer Company, Inc., and
Carr/Sharp Management; © Warren Faidley/
International Stock; FPG International; G.L. French/H.
Armstrong Roberts; Reproduced with permission by
Graceland, Elvis Presley Enterprises Division; Kit
Kittle; © Ken Lax/Stock Shop; Dick Luria/FPG
International; Mauritius/Stock Shop; Movie Still
Archives; Photo Researchers; © Martin Rogers 1993/
FPG International; Don Spiro/Stock Shop; Superstock;
© Peter Tenzer/International Stock; © Tom Tracy/
Stock Shop; UPI/Bettmann

The publisher would like to thank the following companies:
AeroMexico, Air Canada, American Express, Banco de
Bogota, Bank of Montreal, Bank of Taiwan, British
Airways Plc, Ferrari North America, Inc., The Fuji
Bank, Limited, General Motors, Japan Airlines, Major
League Baseball Properties, Rolls-Royce Motor Cars
Inc., United States Coast Guard, United States Olympic
Committee, The Walt Disney Company©

Students can buy a cassette or CD which
contains a recording of the texts and dialogues in this book.

The *Sun King* is a cruise ship. It is sailing around the Caribbean. There are a lot of tourists on the ship. Most of them are from the United States, but some of them are from Canada and Latin America. It's the seventh day of the cruise, and their ship is sailing from Venezuela to Barbados. All of the passengers and most of the crew are on deck for the captain's party.

A: Hello. My name's Pierre Lafontaine. I'm from Montreal.
B: Hi. I'm Heather Hillman.
A: Where do you come from?
B: I come from Montgomery.
A: Montgomery. Where's that?
B: It's in Alabama…. Haven't you heard of Alabama?
A: Oh, yes, of course, Alabama. It's in the South. I've never been to the South.

Questions
What is the *Sun King*?
What is the *Sun King* doing?
Are all of the passengers from the United States?
Ask, "How many of them…?"
Where are the others from?
Is it the first day of the cruise?
Ask, "Which day?"
Where's the ship?
Where are the passengers?
Why are they there?

C: What a terrible party!
D: Oh, really? Do you think so?
C: Yes, I do. Oh, by the way, my name's Marianne Wilson.
D: I'm Tom Gray. Nice to meet you.
C: I work in a bank. What do you do?
D: Well, I'm captain of this ship. It's my party.
C: Oh, I'm so sorry!
D: That's OK. No problem.

E: Would you like another drink?
F: What?
E: Would you like another drink?
F: Oh, yes, please. I'd like some orange juice.
E: With ice?
F: No, thanks.

Exercise 1

BOARDING CARD   THE SUN KING

Last name	First name	Middle initial
Nationality	Date of birth	Occupation
Address		Phone
Signature		Date

All of the passengers had to fill out this boarding card. Ask somebody these questions and fill out the card for him or her.
What's your last name?
What's your first name?
What's your middle initial?
When were you born?
What nationality are you?
What do you do?
Where do you live?

Exercise 2

This is a first-class cabin on the *Sun King*. There are two beds, and there's a shower.

Describe the cabin.

W.C.
bathtub/ shower
closet
chair
telephone
2 beds
dressing table

Exercise 3

SUN KING ITINERARY

Itinerary

Day of the week	Day of the cruise	Location
Saturday	1st	Miami
Monday	3rd	Jamaica
Wednesday	5th	Curaçao
Thursday	6th	Venezuela
Saturday	8th	Barbados
Sunday	9th	Martinique
Monday	10th	Virgin Islands
Tuesday	11th	Puerto Rico
Thursday	13th	Dominican Republic
Saturday	15th	Miami

Where have they been? When did they go there? Where haven't they been yet? Where are they going? When are they going there?

Jade: 212-332-1506. That's it.
Message: Thank you for calling XYZ Records Incorporated. You are in a call waiting system. Please hold. Your call is very important to us. As soon as an operator is free, we'll talk with you…
Operator: XYZ. Can I help you?
Jade: I'd like to speak to James Singh, please.
Operator: Which department?
Jade: Accounting.
Operator: Please hold. I'm connecting you.

Message: Thank you for calling Lemon Computers. If you are calling from a touch-tone phone, and you know the extension number you require, you may dial it now, or at any time during this message. For sales and marketing, press 1 now. For customer service, press 3 now. For all other inquiries press 0, or stay on the line and someone will assist you shortly. Thank you for calling Lemon Computers.
Operator: Lemon Computers. May I help you?
Tomas: Can I speak to Simon Hertz, please?
Operator: One moment.

Paula: Let's see. I press zero first, then the area code and number…. What's the area code for Honolulu? Right. 808. 0-808-725-9316.
Operator: Operator.
Paula: Hello, this is a collect call.
Operator: What name?
Paula: Sinewski. Paula Sinewski.
Operator: Can you spell that, please?
Paula: That's S-I-N-E-W-S-K-I.
Operator. Just a moment. Please hold.
Paula: Thank you.

James Singh
  Accounting
Laura Nazarian
  Sales
Angel Lopez
  Marketing
Donna Steinbeck
  Advertising

sales and
  marketing 1
customer
  service 3
advertising 5
public
  relations 9

Can I…?
May I…?
I'd like to….

Paula Sinewski
Cathy Fitzgerald
William Bendix
Steven McQueen
Sarah Hope
Shireen Jabarri
Anita Vineyard

Honolulu 808
El Paso 915
St. Louis 314
Buffalo 716

DIRECTORY ASSISTANCE

In the United States and Canada, you dial the area code, then **555-1212** for directory assistance.
For example: You want to find a number in San Francisco. The area code for San Francisco is 415. You dial 415-**555-1212**.

🎧 Listening

When you call directory assistance, you hear a recorded message. Listen to these five conversations. Write the city and the telephone number on the chart for conversations two to five.

CITY & CODE		TELEPHONE #
1. Minneapolis	(612)	334-9045
2.	(415)	
3.	(305)	
4.	(617)	
5.	(312)	

Fizz is fantastic!

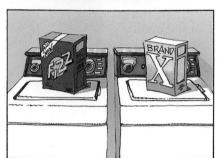

Brian Humble: Meet Mr. and Mrs. Lopez of San Antonio, Texas. They have three young children, and they have to do a lot of wash. There are two piles of dirty clothes on this table. With this pile we're going to use new *Fizz*, and with that pile we're going to use another leading detergent. We have two identical washing machines here. The only difference is *Fizz*. While the machines are working, let's have some coffee.

Brian: OK, both machines have stopped, and Mr. Lopez has taken the clothes out. Well, Mr. Lopez, what do you think?

Mr. L.: Well, we washed these clothes in *Fizz* and those clothes in the other detergent.

Brian: Can you see any difference?

Mr. L.: I sure can! These clothes over here are much cleaner. And they're whiter and softer than those over there.

Brian: These clothes? We washed these clothes with new *Fizz!*

Mrs. L.: That's right, Brian. It's really much better than our usual detergent. Our clothes have never been cleaner than this!

Brian: So, which detergent are you going to use from now on?

Mr. L.: New *Fizz*, of course. It's the best detergent we've ever used!

is best at the laundromat, too!

A lot of people don't have washing machines. They do their wash at a laundromat.

Instructions:
1. Measure Fizz into the machine.
2. Load clothes into the machine. Do not overload.
3. Select water temperature—hot, warm, or cold.
4. Insert ten quarters in the coin slot.
5. Clothes are ready in 30 minutes.

Exercise
While you're waiting at the laundromat, you can have a cup of coffee. Write instructions for the coffee machine.

It's time now for our "Olympic Update," coming to you live by satellite from the Olympic Games. Here's our reporter, Pat Sweeney.

This is the Olympic swimming pool, at the center of the Olympic complex. The most important event today was certainly the women's 200-meter freestyle competition. An American, Sierra Kennedy, was first and won the gold medal. She swam the 200 meters in a new world's record of 1 minute 56 seconds. The United States won two gold medals yesterday and three the day before, so in the first three days of the Olympic Games the American team has won six gold medals.

Javelin
Here you see Jack Lumber from Canada. This morning he won the men's javelin final. On his first try he threw the javelin over 100 meters. Nobody has ever done that before—a new world's record. Unfortunately, there was nearly a terrible accident in the javelin event. Harvey Jones, the American competitor, slipped when he was throwing his javelin, and it hit a judge in the foot. Luckily, the judge was fine.

Gymnastics
Here we are in the Olympic Gymnasium. Olga Ivanov, the fifteen-year-old Russian gymnast, has just finished her routine. We're waiting for the results now.
And here they are! She has an average of 9.5 points. That's the best score today! Olga's won the gold medal.

Exercise 1

Here are some Olympic gold medal winners:

Men's Discus Throw:
Romas Ubartas, Lithuania 65.12 m.
Romas Ubartas from Lithuania won the men's discus throw. He threw the discus 65.12 meters.

Women's Swimming (50-m. freestyle):
Yang Wenyi, China 24.79 sec.
Yang Wenyi from China won the women's 50-meter freestyle. She swam 50 meters in 24.79 seconds.

Make sentences for:

Women's 400-m. Dash:
Marie-José Pérec, France 48.83 sec.

Men's Swimming (1,500-m. freestyle):
Keiren Perkins, Australia 14 min. 43.48 sec.

Women's Running High Jump:
Heine Henkel, Germany 2.02 meters

Men's Long Jump:
Carl Lewis, U.S.A. 8.67 meters

Women's Discus Throw:
Maritza Marten, Cuba 70.06 meters

Women's Swimming (200-m. breaststroke):
Kyoko Iwasaki, Japan 2 min. 26.65 sec.

High jump

We're waiting for the last jumper. Ted Kelly from Great Britain is going to jump. The bar is at 2.30 meters.

Now he's beginning his last try.

And he's jumped!

Oooh! He's crashed into the bar!

He's landing. The bar's fallen. Is he hurt?

No, no, he's all right. He's getting up and walking away, but he's a very disappointed man.

Exercise 2

A. He's going to lift it. **B.** He's lifting it. **C.** He's lifted it.

Make sentences:

A. . . . jump. **B. . . . .** **C. . . . .**

 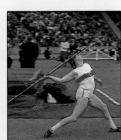 

A. . . . throw. **B. . . . .** **C. . . . .**

5 Waiting for a friend

Mrs. Katz: What's the matter, Debbie?

Debbie: I'm waiting for a letter from Nick. It wasn't here yesterday, and it isn't here today either.

Mrs. Katz: Don't worry, honey. It'll be here tomorrow.

Debbie: Will it? I don't know.

The next day

Debbie: Mom! It's here! And Nick's coming to Pittsburgh!

Mrs. Katz: Oh, really? When?

Debbie: He'll be here next Monday.

Mrs Katz: What time will he be here? You have classes on Monday.

Debbie: He'll be on the 7:40 train. Oh, Mom, can he stay with us?

Mrs. Katz: Well, I don't know…. Oh, OK. Sure. I've heard so much about him. I'd like to meet him.

The next Monday

Mrs. Katz: Debbie! The train won't be here for ten minutes. Let's get a soda or something.

Debbie: No, thanks, Mom. You guys get a soda.

Mrs. Katz: All right. Where will you be?

Debbie: I'll be right here.

Ten minutes later

Mrs. Katz: Well, the train's late.

Debbie: It'll be here soon. Uh, Mom…can you and Sarah wait in the coffee shop?

Mrs. Katz: Why, dear?

Debbie: I want to say hello to Nick on my own. Is that OK?

Mrs. Katz: Sure. But we've just had a soda. We'll be in the bookstore right over there.

Debbie: Thanks, Mom. I won't be long.

Exercise

A. He'll be here tomorrow.
B. *He won't be here tomorrow.*
C. *Will he be here tomorrow?*

A. They'll be here next week.
B. . . . .
C. . . . .

A. . . . .
B. . . . .
C. Will you be here next year?

🎧 Listening

Listen to the station announcements. The trains will be late.
When will they be here? Complete the chart.

ARRIVAL FROM	TIME DUE	WILL ARRIVE	TRACK NUMBER
Philadelphia	6:45 pm		
Cincinnati	7:15 pm		
Chicago / Cleveland	7:40 pm		
St. Louis	8:20 pm		

Monday morning

Dan: What's the matter, honey?

Rosie: Oh, I don't know.

Dan: Come on! Something's the matter! What is it?

Rosie: It's just life. It's so boring.

Dan: It's not that bad. We have two wonderful children.

Rosie: That's right. We do. And we never have any time with them.

Dan: Well, we both have to work, hon. We need the money.

Rosie: OK, but it's all right for you. I'll leave in five minutes, but you'll be here all day. I won't be home till six.

Dan: Sure, but your day will be interesting and you'll meet people. I'll be here in front of the computer screen all day. I won't talk to anyone.

Rosie: You're a computer programmer, Dan. That's your job. You're lucky. You can work at home.

Dan: Yeah, but you like your job, Rosie. You really do.

Rosie: What! Who will I meet today? Tell me that. What will I do? I'll tell you, Dan. I'll get on the same train, then I'll go

to the same office. I'll speak to the same boring people and I'll listen to the same stupid jokes. I'll get the same train home, then I'll get home and help the kids with their homework…

Dan: I'll cook dinner, honey. I always do.

Rosie: Yeah? But I'll wash the dishes. Then we'll watch TV again. You'll be tired and we won't talk. Then we'll do the same tomorrow. What a life! Today, tomorrow, this week, next week, this month, next month, next year—forever!

Dan: It's just Monday morning, Rosie. You'll feel OK tomorrow.

Rosie: Will I?

Her Monday
Rosie O'Connell, reporter
7:30 catch the train
8:30 arrive at the office
10:00 meet the president
12:00 have lunch with Madonna
3:00 interview Janet Jackson
4.00 call Stephen Speilberg
5:00 catch the train
6:00 arrive home
7:30 help the kids with their homework
8:00 have dinner
9:00 watch TV
11:00 go to bed

His Monday
Dan O'Connell, programmer
7:15 drive Rosie to the train station
7:45 wash the dishes
10:00 open the mail
10:30 do the wash
12:00 work on the computer
2:30 fax Microworld Computers
3:00 pick kids up at school
4:00 work on the computer
5:45 meet Rosie at the train station
7:30 cook dinner
8:00 have dinner
9:00 read to the kids
10:15 go to bed

Exercise 1
What will she do at 7:30?
She'll catch the train.

Make questions and answers about Rosie.

Exercise 2
When will he drive Rosie to the train station?
He'll drive Rosie to the train station at 7:15.

Write questions and answers about Dan.

Interviewer: Good evening, and welcome to Channel 35 News. A 66-year-old Monterey man, Mr. Walter Busby, is in the studio with us. Mr. Busby is a retired bank clerk. Tomorrow morning he will begin a fantastic voyage. He and his wife, Betty, are going to sail from Monterey, California, to Australia. That's 7,000 miles across the ocean—in a small motorboat.

Int: Now, Walter…

Waldo: Please, call me Waldo. All my friends call me Waldo.

Int: All right, Waldo. Why are you doing this?

Waldo: Well, I haven't seen my son for ten years. He lives in Australia. And we've never seen our grandchildren.

Int: But your boat isn't very big, Waldo. Will it get to Australia?

Waldo: Oh, yes. I think so. It'll get there all right. It'll take a long time, of course. But we're not in a hurry. I just retired, you see. And we'll stop on the way.

Int: Where will you stop? Do you know?

Waldo: Oh, yes. We have a map. Here it is. We'll stop at several places. We'll need food and gas.

Int: Ah, yes. Food. What'll you do about food?

Waldo: No problem. We'll catch fish.

Int: I see. And water?

Waldo: That won't be a problem either. It'll rain. It rains a lot at sea, you know.

Int: Will you take a radio with you?

Waldo: No, no, no. We never listen to the radio. We don't like pop music. We like some peace and quiet. We'll take a lot of books.

Int: Well actually, I meant a two-way radio. How will you navigate? Will you use a compass?

Waldo: A compass? No. We won't need a compass or a radio. We'll navigate by the sun and stars. I got a book from the library.

Int: Well, good luck, Waldo. You'll certainly need it.

Exercise

Look at the map. Which places will they visit?

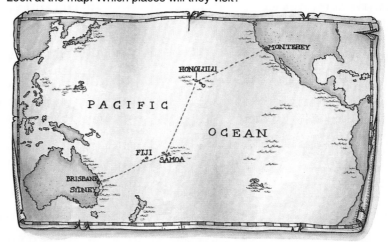

🎧 Listening

Listen to the news report.

1. Where are Mr. and Mrs. Busby now?
2. What time did they leave Monterey?
3. What happened to the boat?
4. What did the helicopter do?
5. What are the Busbys looking for?

IT HAPPENED TO ME - - - - - -

We all spend 30% of our lives asleep in bed. This week we asked readers for letters about sleep and dreams.

A SHORT FLIGHT

Last year I had to fly to London for business. I can't sleep on airplanes, so my doctor gave me some sleeping pills. I got onto the plane, sat down, and took two pills. We took off and a few minutes later I was asleep. When I woke, the flight attendant was shaking my arm. I was the only passenger on the plane. "Those pills were strong," I thought. I went to the baggage claim area. I couldn't see my bags anywhere. I went to the information desk, and asked about my bags. "Which flight were you on?" asked the desk clerk.

"The flight from New York—743," I said.

"But you didn't go anywhere, ma'am. Your aircraft had a problem with the engines and it came back. This is New York!"

Wilhemina C. Williams
Paterson, New Jersey

SLEEPWALKER

My kid sister often walked in her sleep. One night I woke up suddenly. My sister was walking out of our room with her eyes closed. I got up and followed her to the kitchen. She opened the fridge and took out some chocolate cheesecake. Her eyes never opened. She ate it, then went back to our room. I told her in the morning, but she didn't believe me. "Look in the mirror," I said. There was chocolate all around her mouth and nose!

Candi Faulkner
Oxford, Mississippi

WHAT A NIGHTMARE!

I once had a terrible nightmare. I dreamed I was in a hotel room on the 40th floor. The hotel was on fire. Smoke was coming under the door. I couldn't open the window. I hit it with a chair, but I couldn't break it. The room got hotter and hotter and the smoke got thicker and thicker. "This is the end," I thought. Then I heard a crash. Right then, I woke up. I was at home, in my own bed, in my own room, and the room really was full of smoke. The window was open, and a fire fighter was climbing into the room. He rescued me. My apartment was on fire!

Jackson Burns
Seattle, Washington

HOW ABOUT YOU?

1. Most people need eight hours of sleep. How about you?
2. Some people need an alarm clock. How about you?
3. Some people can sleep anywhere—in a chair, on the floor, on a bus. How about you?
4. Some people always remember their dreams. How about you?
5. Some people dream in black and white, some people dream in color. How about you?
6. Most people have had a nightmare. How about you?

A: Can I help you?
B: Yes, thank you. I have a terrible headache.
A: How long have you had it?
B: About two or three hours.
A: Well, try these pills. Take two every four hours.
B: Thank you very much.
A: You're welcome.

headache
stomachache
backache
earache
sore throat

pills
capsules
tablets
drops
throat lozenges

C: Could I have a box of throat lozenges, please?
D: With antiseptic or without?
C: With.
D: There you go. Will that be all?
C: Yes, that's all. Sorry, I only have a fifty-dollar bill.
D: OK, out of fifty. Here's your change.
C: Thank you.
D: You're welcome.

a box of throat
lozenges
antiseptic/
without
a bottle of vitamin C
tablets
large/small
a tube of toothpaste
with fluoride/
without
a bar of soap
large/small
a can of antiseptic
spray
large/small

E: Could you fill this prescription, please?
F: Sure. Do you want to wait?
E: How long will it take?
F: It'll be ready in about twenty minutes.
E: Oh. I'll come back later.
F: All right. It'll be waiting.
E: Should I pay now or later?
F: Later will be fine.

about 20 minutes
a few minutes
a moment
about an hour
half an hour

Exercise

Look at the containers on the left. Match the words to the containers. Remember, some words will match with two or more containers!

Superstar

Maria-Donna: Come in!
Gary: Yes, Ms. Baloney?
Maria-Donna: No, no, Gary! I don't want you.
Gary: Who do you want, Ms. Baloney?
Maria-Donna: I want Marvin, and I want him right away.
Gary: OK. I'll go and find him.

Maria-Donna: Ah, Marvin!
Marvin: Did you want to see me, ma'am?
Maria-Donna: Yes. I wanted to see you twenty minutes ago.
Marvin: I'm sorry. I was in the garage.
Maria-Donna: I want a car this afternoon.
Marvin: Which car do you want to take? The stretch limo, the Rolls-Royce, or the Ferrari?
Maria-Donna: The stretch limo.
Marvin: Where do you want to go, ma'am?
Maria-Donna: The recording studio.
Marvin: What time?
Maria-Donna: The recording session begins at two. We'll leave here at one-thirty.

Maria-Donna: OK, Brandon. Can you hear me?
Brandon: Sure.
Maria-Donna: I want you to play electric piano on this one.
Brandon: No problem.
Maria-Donna: And I want Jared to play acoustic guitar. I want him to play real loudly, OK?
Brandon: You got it.
Maria-Donna: And find Tania and Sophie. I want them to sing doo-wops.
Brandon: Excuse me?
Maria-Donna: You know, the chorus. Doo-wop-di-diddy-diddy-dum-di-do.

Exercise 1

I wanted to do something.
What did you want to do?
1. They wanted to go somewhere.
2. He wanted to buy something.
3. We wanted to meet someone.
4. She wanted to eat something.
5. I wanted to see someone.

Exercise 2

She/them/make dinner.
She wants them to make dinner.
1. He/me/call him.
2. I/him/help me.
3. They/her/clean the room.
4. My parents/me/learn English.
5. The police/them/stop.
6. She/me/dance.
7. The teacher/us/do our homework.

Exercise 3

When I was young, my parents wanted me to be a doctor. They wanted me to work hard.

What did your	father	want you to do?
	mother	
	parents	
	teachers	

What did you want to do?

Look, feel, taste, sound, smell

A: I like your car, Jackie.
B: Oh, you do? I've only had it for a week.
A: It looks very expensive.
B: Really? I guess new ones are expensive, but this one's used.
A: It is? It doesn't look like a used car. It looks brand new.

C: Brrr! It feels cold in here.
D: It does?
C: Yes, really cold. Is the heat on?
D: Yes, it is. It'll feel warmer in a minute.

E: Waiter!
F: Yes, sir.
E: These vegetables aren't fresh!
F: But they *are* fresh, sir.
E: Well, they don't taste fresh to me. I want you to get the manager.

G: I'd like you to listen to my new stereo, Eduardo. Does it sound all right?
H: Yes, it sounds fine to me.
G: I think the bass is too loud.
H: No, it sounds perfect. It sounds better than mine.

I: Have you changed your perfume?
J: Yes, why? Do you like it?
I: Yes, it smells wonderful. What is it?
J: It's *Roseanne* by Devlon.
I: It smells expensive. Is it?
J: I don't know. It was a present.

Exercise 1

This one's used.	*It is?*
I like your car.	*You do?*
It feels cold.	*It does?*
It doesn't taste fresh.	*It doesn't?*

1. They're very old.
2. I don't like coffee.
3. It sounds perfect.
4. It doesn't smell expensive.
5. This one's mine.

Exercise 2

How do these things
taste/sound/look/smell/feel?
Fresh coffee smells wonderful.

Make sentences.
fresh coffee/cigar smoke/cat fur/leather
seats/silk/wet dogs/fresh bread/
expensive ties/freeways/canned peas/
stale cookies/stale fish/Caribbean
beaches/roses/old sneakers

A science-fiction story

The spaceship flew around the new planet several times. The planet was blue and green. They couldn't see the surface of the planet because there were too many white clouds. Then the spaceship descended slowly through the clouds and landed in the middle of a green forest. The two astronauts put on their space suits, opened the door, climbed carefully down the ladder, and stepped onto the planet.

The woman looked at a small control unit on her arm. "It's OK," she said to the man. "We can breathe the air. It's a mixture of oxygen and nitrogen." Both of them took off their helmets and breathed deeply.

They looked at everything carefully. All the plants and animals looked new and strange. They couldn't find any intelligent life.

After several hours, they returned to their spaceship. Everything looked normal. The man turned on the controls, but nothing happened. "Something's wrong," he said. "I don't understand. The engines aren't working." He switched on the computer, but that didn't work either. "Eve," he said, "we're stuck here. We can't take off!"

"Don't worry, Adam," she replied. "They'll rescue us soon."

It's too hot!

In the hotel coffee shop
(7:30 PM)

Mike: Come on, Kim. Hurry up and finish your coffee. We have to catch a taxi to the airport. We'll be late.

Kim: I can't hurry. This coffee's too hot for me to drink.

Mike: Why don't you put some cold milk in it?

Kim: Milk? I don't take milk in my coffee. Oh, OK, OK.

Mike: Is it cool enough for you to drink now?

Kim: Yes, but it tastes awful!

At the airport (8:00 PM)

Kim: Oh, no! The Global counter looks a mile away!

Mike: Ooh! What did you put in these suitcases? Rocks?

Kim: Only clothes. Why? Are they heavy?

Mike: Yes, they are.

Kim: The taxi driver managed to carry them.

Mike: Well, they're too heavy for me to carry, and I don't see any luggage carts.

Kim: Well, I'm not strong enough to help you. Porter! Over here, please.

On the plane (9:00 PM)

Kim: Oh, Mike. I didn't tell you. My sister called this morning.

Mike: Oh? Which one? Tiffany?

Kim: Yes. She wants to get married.

Mike: Married! She isn't old enough to get married. She's only seventeen. Who does she want to marry?

Kim: Marc McIntosh.

Mike: Marc McIntosh, the actor? I can't believe it! He's too old for her. He's over sixty!

Kim: I know, but she loves him.

In the hotel coffee shop

At the airport

On the plane

At their destination

At their destination (11:00 PM)

Kim: Oh, no! There goes the last bus!

Mike: Well, let's walk to the highway and catch a different bus.

Kim: It's a mile away! That's too far for me to walk. Let's take a taxi.

Mike: Another taxi! We aren't rich enough to go everywhere by taxi.

Kim: Mike, haven't you forgotten something?

Mike: What?

Kim: We have three suitcases. Do you really want to walk?

Mike: You're right. Taxi!

Exercise 1

He can't lift it. It's very heavy.
It's too heavy for him to lift.
1. They can't drink it. It's very hot.
2. She can't buy it. It's too expensive.
3. He can't answer it. It's very hard.
4. We can't see it. It's very small.

Exercise 2

Can he lift the boxes?
No, he isn't strong enough to lift them.
1. Can you touch the ceiling? (tall)
2. Can they buy that house? (rich)
3. Can she understand the questions? (smart)
4. Can that cat catch the bird? (quick)

Two phone calls

Vicki: Hello?

Randy: Vicki? Is that you?

Vicki: Uh-huh. Who's this?

Randy: It's Randy.

Vicki: Randy? Randy who?

Randy: What do you mean, "Randy who?" Randy Dixon, of course.

Vicki: Oh, Randy, I'm sorry.

Randy: Yes. We had a date last night. Where were you? I waited for two hours.

Vicki: Oh, I'm sorry, Randy. I couldn't come.

Randy: Couldn't come! Why not?

Vicki: Well, I had to wash my hair.

Randy: Wash your hair! Why didn't you call me?

Vicki: I wanted to call you, but—uh—I—uh—couldn't remember your phone number.

Randy: It's in the phone book.

Vicki: Yes, of course, but—uh—I couldn't remember your last name.

Randy: Oh…. But why did you have to wash your hair last night?

Vicki: Well, I had to do it last night because I'm going to see a play tonight.

Randy: To see a play? With who?

Vicki: George. George McQueen, my boss's son.

Randy: I see.

Vicki: He asked me yesterday, and I couldn't say no.

Questions

Who's calling?
Who's answering the phone?
Did they have a date?
Ask, "When?"
Why couldn't she come?
Did she want to call him?
Why didn't she call him?
Is his number in the phone book?
Why couldn't she find it?
Did she have to wash her hair?
Ask, "Why?"
Is she going to the theater with Randy?
Ask, "Who…with?"
When did George ask her?
Why did she say yes?

🎧 Listening

Listen to the next phone call. Who is the manager talking to? Now listen again and check (✓) true or false.

	true	false
1. Someone is calling from the First State Bank.	☐	☐
2. The manager sent a letter.	☐	☐
3. She hasn't called before.	☐	☐
4. She phoned in the afternoon.	☐	☐
5. He had to see his dentist.	☐	☐
6. Mr. Trump wrote a check for $1,000.	☐	☐
7. Mr. Trump had $102.95 in his account.	☐	☐
8. Mr. Sikorski's number is 848-3592.	☐	☐

Sergeant: Good morning. Are you the new janitor of the building?

Corona: Janitor? No, not me. I want to join the army, man.

Sergeant: What! You! In the army?

Corona: Yeah. I want to be a soldier. This is the Army Recruiting Office, isn't it?

Sergeant: Well…uh…yes. Sit down, son.

Corona: Thanks, man.

Sergeant: Now, why do you want to be a soldier, Mr. …uh…what's your name, son?

Corona: Corona. Frankie Corona. Well, I saw the commercial on TV last night. It looked pretty good. Vacations, money, travel, education, a pension….

Sergeant: I see. Yes, it's a good life in the army.

Corona: Terrific!

Sergeant: Now, do you have any questions?

Corona: Let's see. Yes. Will I have to get a haircut?

Sergeant: Oh yes, you'll have to get a haircut—and wear a uniform.

Corona: A uniform? I've never had to wear a uniform before.

Sergeant: Oh yes, and you'll have to obey orders. But you won't have to clean latrines, ha-ha.

Corona: What are latrines?

Sergeant: Toilets. I've never had to clean toilets.

Corona: What about the work? Will I have to work hard?

Sergeant: Oh, yes. You'll have to work hard, all right.

Corona: Hmm. And what about education?

Sergeant: Oh, yes. There are a lot of opportunities. Maybe you'll be a computer programmer or a communications expert one day.

Corona: OK. I'd like to join.

Sergeant: All right. Just sign here, Frankie.

Corona: There you go, man—Frankie Corona.

Sergeant: Corona!

Corona: Huh?

Sergeant: Stand up. Stand up straight, Corona. Now, march! Left, right, left, right. You're in the army now!

Exercise

A friend is going into the army in your country.
What will he/she have to do?
What won't he/she have to do?

Write six sentences.

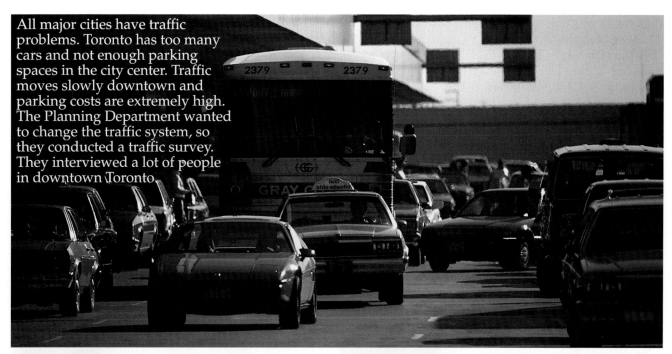

All major cities have traffic problems. Toronto has too many cars and not enough parking spaces in the city center. Traffic moves slowly downtown and parking costs are extremely high. The Planning Department wanted to change the traffic system, so they conducted a traffic survey. They interviewed a lot of people in downtown Toronto.

1
David Chang is fifty-eight. He learned to drive when he was eighteen. He's been able to drive for forty years. He lives about twenty miles away. He always comes downtown by car.

3
Douglas MacKenzie is twenty. He's had a lot of driving lessons. He's taken the driving test three times, but he hasn't been able to pass the test yet. He lives near the city center, and works in a mall downtown. He usually walks to work.

2
Layla Patel is twenty-five. She's been able to drive for six years, but she doesn't have a car. She hasn't been able to save enough money. She lives about thirty-five miles away. She always comes into town by train.

4
Mr. and Mrs. Hawkins are both over sixty-five. They've never been able to drive. They've never learned. They don't live far from downtown, and they occasionally come downtown by streetcar.

Complete the survey for Layla Patel (2), Douglas MacKenzie (3), and Mr. and Mrs. Hawkins (4).

🎧 **Listening**

Listen to the next two interviews and complete the survey for (5) and (6).

TRAFFIC AND PUBLIC TRANSIT SURVEY: METROPOLITAN TORONTO

	WHAT'S YOUR NAME?	HOW OLD ARE YOU?	CAN YOU DRIVE?	HOW LONG HAVE YOU BEEN ABLE TO DRIVE?	WHERE DO YOU LIVE?	HOW DO YOU GET DOWNTOWN?
1	David Chang	58	Yes	40 years	20 miles away	by car
2						
3						
4						
5						
6						

Principal: Why do you want to study computer programming?

Robbie: Well, I lost my job last month, and I haven't been able to find another one.

Principal: I see. Do you have any money?

Robbie: Well, some, and my girlfriend will be able to help me.

Principal: Good. The course costs $2,500.

Robbie: *Whew!* Will I be able to find a job as a computer programmer?

Principal: Oh, sure! You'll be able to get a good job and make lots of money…. Please sign here.

Mrs. Wood: This is the room. Do you like it?

Lois: It's very nice. Is it quiet? I'm a writer.

Mrs. W: You'll be able to work with no problem. There's almost no noise here.

Lois: Will I be able to use the kitchen?

Mrs. W: Yes, of course.

Lois: Fine. It looks good. *(Crash!)* What's that?

Mrs. W: Oh, that's just our neighbor. He works on old cars. *(Crash!)* He's usually quiet.

Manager: Have a seat, Jim. You work in the mail room, right?

Jim: That's right. I want to transfer to the International Sales Division.

Manager: Why do you want to join the International Division, Jim?

Jim: Well, I don't really. I just want to travel to Latin America.

Manager: How good is your Spanish?

Jim: Spanish? I've never been able to learn Spanish.

Manager: Well, what will you be able to do in the International Sales Division?

Jim: I don't know. But I won't be able to work very hard. I have a bad back.

Look at this:

He'll be able to find a job.
He won't be able to work hard.
Will she be able to write in the room?

Exercise

Complete this conversation using *be able to find.*

Applicant: I want to teach English in South America. • • • a job in Bogotá?

Interviewer: Did you graduate from college?

Applicant: Oh, yes. I have a master's degree in ESL.

Interviewer: Then • • • a job at our Bogotá center.

Applicant: What about living arrangements? • • • an apartment?

Interviewer: Well, that's hard. • • • (not) • • • an apartment right away, but • • • one after a few months.

Checks and money

A: Next! Good morning.
B: Good morning. I'd like to cash this check, please.
A: OK, $200. Oh! You haven't signed it.
B: Really? Oh, I'm sorry. There you go.
A: How would you like the money?
B: Twenties, please. Oh, and could I have twenty dollars in smaller bills?
A: Sure. 20, 40, 60, 80, 100, 120, 140, 160, 180, 190, 195, 6, 7, 8, 9, 200.

$200 (9 x $20/ 1 x $10/ 1 x $5/ 5 x $1)
$100 (4 x $20/ 2 x $10)
$50 (5 x $10)
$200 (5 x $20/ 20 x $5)
$500 (9 x $50/ 5 x $10)

C: I'd like to get this, but I don't have enough cash on me. Do you take traveler's checks?
D: Yes, of course.
C: Good. Here you are.
D: Thank you. I'll need some identification too.
C: Sure. Is my driver's license all right?
D: Yes, that's fine. Just sign and date it. I have a stamp with the store's name.

traveler's checks
driver's license

American Express
student ID card

Visa
passport

E: Hello. Can I help you?
F: Thank you. My name is Toshiko Akiyama. I'm expecting a transfer from my bank in Tokyo.
E: Let me see. Here it is. Akiyama, $2,000 from the Fuji Bank in Tokyo. Do you have your driver's license with you?
F: No, but I have my passport. Will that be all right?
E: Yes, of course.

Toshiko Akiyama/ $2,000/Fuji Bank/ Tokyo

Jung Lee/ $3,000/The Bank of Korea/Seoul

Monique Lanois/ $1,000/Banque de Montreal/Quebec

Juan Enrique Botero/ $4,000/Banco de Bogotá/Bogotá

Questionnaire

Ask another student these questions.

1. What's the exchange rate between your currency and the U.S. dollar?
2. American bills are all the same size and the same color. What about your country's currency?
3. Is it better for bills to be different colors and sizes? Why?/Why not?
4. In the U.S.A. and Canada, most stores accept traveler's checks. What about your country?
5. The largest U.S. coin is the dollar. The smallest bill is one dollar. What about your country's currency?
6. In some parts of the U.S.A. and Canada, stores will add sales tax to the prices (e.g., Florida sales tax is 6%). Are there sales taxes in your country? Does the price in the store include sales tax, or does the store add the tax to the price?

Mr. Harris: I'd like to make a reservation for the excursion to Egypt leaving July 16.

Travel Agent: The one at the Cleopatra Hotel?

Mr. Harris: That's it. How far is it from the hotel to the beach?

Travel Agent: About a two-minute walk.

Mr. Harris: Good. How hot is it in Egypt in July?

Travel Agent: About 32° Centigrade. That's 90° Fahrenheit.

Guide: And that is the Great Pyramid.

Mr. Harris: Oh, yes. It looks very high!

Guide: It's about 137 meters high.

Mr. Harris: How long are the sides?

Guide: They're 230 meters long.

Mr. Harris: *Wow!* How old is it?

Guide: It's almost four-and-a-half thousand years old.

Sailor: We're going through the Suez Canal now.

Mr. Harris: It doesn't look very wide. How wide is it?

Sailor: About 60 meters wide and 160 kilometers long.

Mr. Harris: Really? This is a big ship. How deep is the canal?

Sailor: The average depth is about 10 meters.

Guide: Hello, Mr. Harris. Are you coming on the bus trip to Cairo tomorrow?

Mr. Harris: Yes. How far is it?

Guide: It's about 150 kilometers.

Mr. Harris: How long will it take to get there?

Guide: About three hours.

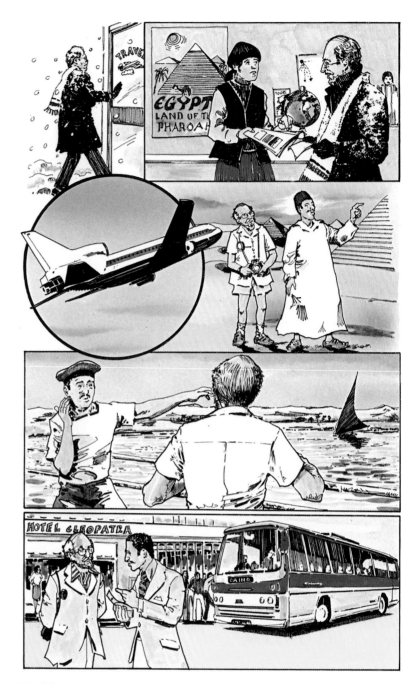

FLORIDA	MIAMI	KEY WEST	PALM BEACH	ORLANDO	TAMPA	DAYTONA BEACH	TALLAHASSEE
MIAMI		160	74	232	261	258	480
KEY WEST	160		223	390	399	415	637
PALM BEACH	74	223		170	203	197	427
ORLANDO	232	390	170		84	54	260
TAMPA	261	399	203	84		153	245
DAYTONA BEACH	258	415	197	54	153		239
TALLAHASSEE	480	637	427	260	245	239	

Exercise 1

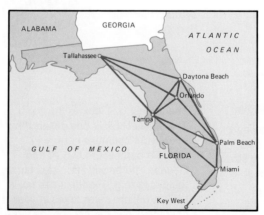

Look at the map and the chart.
How far is it from Miami to Key West?
It's 160 miles.

Write seven sentences like this.

Exercise 2

Maria
height: 1 m. 62 cm./5 ft. 3 in.
age: 30

João
height: 1 m. 85 cm./6 ft. 1 in.
age: 27

How old is Maria?
She's thirty.

How tall is she?
She's one meter, sixty-two centimeters./
She's five three.

Write two questions about João.

Ten years ago, Ford Studebaker had an accident in his car. He was driving quickly and carelessly. After the accident his wife said, "Ford, you're an old man now. You have to drive more slowly, and more carefully." Ford has not had an accident since then. He always drives slowly—very slowly.

But the drivers behind him often get angry. They sometimes have to stop suddenly, and then other cars crash into them. Ford always drives in the middle of the road, and other drivers can't pass him. They sound their horns and flash their lights, because they want Ford to go more quickly. But Ford never notices them, and he never sees the accidents behind him. When he reads about the accidents in the newspaper, he says to his wife, "People drive more carelessly these days. Everybody's in a hurry. I don't understand it!"

Questions

1. Why did Ford have an accident?
2. How does he drive these days?
3. Why do other drivers get angry?
4. What do they want him to do?
5. What does Ford think about drivers these days?

Natasha Terranova is a tennis star. She's one of the best players in the world. She hits the ball hard and fast—harder and faster than any other player. But many people dislike her because she often behaves badly. She sometimes gets very angry. Last year she shouted at the crowd, and broke her racket on the ground during the final of the Texas Championship. She didn't play well and lost. This year she played better and won the final. Unfortunately, she got very angry and behaved worse than last year. She threw her racket at the umpire! She will never be able to play in the Texas Championship again.

Questions

1. How does Natasha hit the ball?
2. Why do some people dislike her?
3. How did she play in last year's final?
4. How did she play in this year's final?
5. How did she behave in this year's final?

Look at this:

slowly…more slowly/slower	well…better	carefully…more carefully	fast…faster
quickly…more quickly/quicker	badly…worse	carelessly…more carelessly	hard…harder

A day off

Al Bellini works for an import-export company in Los Angeles. One morning last summer, Al called his office at nine o'clock. His boss, Ralph Vasquez, answered the phone.

Ralph: Hello. Ralph Vasquez.
Al: Hello, Ralph. This is Al Bellini.
Ralph: Oh, hi, Al. What's up?
Al: I don't think I can come to work today, Ralph.
Ralph: Oh? What's the problem?
Al: I've got a very bad sore throat.
Ralph: Yes, you sound sick.
Al: Yes. I'll stay in bed today, but I'll be able to come tomorrow.
Ralph: That's all right, Al. Stay in bed until you feel well enough to come to work.
Al: Thank you, Ralph. Good-bye.
Ralph: Bye, Al.

Ralph liked Al a lot. At 12:30 he got into his car, drove to a store, and bought some fruit for him. He went to Al's apartment and rang the doorbell. Al's wife, Stella, answered the door.

Stella: Oh, Ralph! Hello! Come in. How are you?
Ralph: Fine, thanks, Stella. I've come to see Al. How is he?
Stella: He doesn't look very well. I wanted him to see the doctor.
Ralph: I'll go in and see him. Hi, Al!
Al: Oh! Hi. Hi, Ralph—uh—uh—have a seat.
Ralph: I've brought some fruit for you, Al.
Al: Thanks a lot, Ralph.
Ralph: Well, I was in the neighborhood anyway. How's your throat?
Al: It seems a little better. I'll be OK tomorrow.
Ralph: Good, good. Take care. Good-bye, Al.
Al: Bye, Ralph. Thanks for coming by.

At three o'clock, Ralph locked his office door and turned on his portable TV. He wanted to watch an important baseball game. It was the Atlanta Braves versus the Los Angeles Dodgers. Both teams were playing well, but neither team could score. The crowd was cheering and booing. It was very exciting.

Then at 3:20, Sam Zapata of the Dodgers hit a home run. Ralph jumped out of his chair. He was very excited. He was smiling happily when suddenly the cameraman focused on the crowd. Ralph's smile disappeared, and he looked very upset. Al Bellini's face, in close-up, was there on the screen. He didn't look sick, and he didn't sound sick. He was smiling happily and cheering wildly.

Applying for a job

BMI
Import-Export Corp. Darien, Connecticut 06820

EMPLOYMENT APPLICATION FORM

Job Export sales representative
Social security no. 423-50-2151
Last name Chandler
First name Paula   **Middle initial** D.
Address 32 Paul Revere Avenue
Lowell, MA 01854

EDUCATION
High School R.W. Emerson High, Lowell, MA
College Suffolk University, Boston, MA
(BA degree in Business Administration)

WORK EXPERIENCE
Computech, Stanford, Connecticut - 4 years
(Sales representative for Mexico & Central America)

LANGUAGES
Spanish

BARNUM COMPUTER GAMES
3024 Arctic Street, Bridgeport, Connecticut 06608

Application for Employment

Job reference: 32/671 BILINGUAL SECRETARY
Social security no.: 036-45-9271
Full name: PAUL ALAN LANIER
Address: 59 CROSBY AVENUE
FAIRFIELD, CT 06430

Education:
FAIRFIELD HIGH SCHOOL, FAIRFIELD, CT

Previous employment:
STANLEY MANUFACTURING, BRIDGEPORT, CT
1 YEAR —ACCOUNTING CLERK
FAIRFIELD HOSPITAL, FAIRFIELD, CT
8 MONTHS — SECRETARY
NEW ENGLAND AUTO SALES, WESTPORT, CT
1 YEAR —SECRETARY

Languages:
FRENCH — EXCELLENT (MY PARENTS ARE FROM QUEBEC)
SPANISH — GOOD

Art Miranda: How do you do? It's Paula Chandler, isn't it?
Paula Chandler: Yes. How do you do?
Art: Have a seat. I'm Art Miranda, and I have your application form here. I just want to check the information.
Paula: Fine, sure.
Art: You're applying for the position of export sales representative, aren't you?
Paula: Yes, I am.
Art: You aren't from Connecticut, are you?
Paula: No, I'm not. I'm from Massachusetts.
Art: You got a bachelor's degree in business administration at college, didn't you?
Paula: Yes, that's right.
Art: But you didn't get a master's degree, did you?
Paula: No, I didn't.
Art: And you have worked in international sales, haven't you?
Paula: Yes, I have. I've been a sales representative in Mexico and Central America.
Art: But you haven't worked in Brazil, have you?
Paula: No, I haven't, but I'd like to.
Art: You can speak Spanish, can't you?
Paula: Yes, I can.
Art: But you can't speak Portuguese, can you?
Paula: No, I can't. But I'd like to learn Portuguese.

Fill in the blanks.

Interviewer: Come in. Have a seat. It's Paul Lanier, isn't it?
Paul Lanier: Yes, that's right.
Int: Well, I've looked over your application. Can I just check the information?
Paul: Yes, of course.
Int: You're applying for a secretarial job, . . .?
Paul: Yes, a bilingual secretarial job.
Int: You aren't from Bridgeport, . . .?
Paul: No, I'm from Fairfield.
Int: And you went to school in Fairfield, . . .?
Paul: That's correct. Fairfield High.
Int: But you didn't go to college, . . .?
Paul: No, I didn't.
Int: You can speak French well, . . .?
Paul: Yes. My parents are French-Canadian.
Int: But you can't speak German, . . .?
Paul: No. No, I can't. But I can speak Spanish.
Int: You've been a secretary for two years, . . .?
Paul: Yes.
Int: But you haven't stayed in one job for much time, . . .?
Paul: No, I haven't. I've worked in some awful places!

Good evening. Our program tonight is about disasters. This year there have been fires, earthquakes, and volcanic eruptions. All our guests tonight have survived disasters.

Hello. I'm Susan Fisher-Diaz. I live in Chicago. I was working in my office on the 28th floor of a skyscraper. I was dictating some letters to my secretary when the fire alarm rang. I rushed out to the elevator, but it wasn't working. The stairs were full of thick smoke. We couldn't go down, so we had to go up to the roof. When we got there some people were waiting calmly. Others were shouting and screaming wildly. A helicopter managed to land on the roof and rescued six of us before the roof collapsed.

My name's Linda Reed. I was on vacation at the Med Club on Patapita, a small island in the South Pacific. I was taking a nap when the volcano erupted. The noise woke me up. I looked out of the window. Everybody was running toward the harbor. I threw on my robe and ran to the harbor too. I managed to get on a cruise ship. It was leaving when the lava hit town.

Hi. My name's Richard Ching. My wife and I were staying with friends in Santa Librada near Los Angeles. We were having dinner when the earthquake began. Everything shook. All the plates and food fell on the floor. We were picking everything up when the ceiling fell in. Fortunately, we were under the table and survived. We had to wait for hours before help arrived.

Exercise

Complete the blanks using the correct form of the verbs in parentheses ( ).

I was . . . (work) in the field next to the house when I . . . (see) it. The tornado was . . . (move) toward me very fast. I . . . (manage) to get into the storm shelter next to the house. When I . . . (come) out two hours later, the house . . . (isn't) there. The tornado just . . . (blow) it away! Fortunately, no one . . . (is) hurt.

A trip to the old country

Minnie Bronson lives in Sweetwater, Texas. She was born in Thetford, in England. When she was eighteen, she married an American soldier and they moved to the United States. That was forty years ago and she's never been back to England since then. She is planning a trip to England. She wrote a letter to her brother. Her nephew, Oliver, replied.

42 Edgehill Road
Thetford, Norfolk
England
October 10th

Dear Aunt Minnie,
Thank you for your letter. What a surprise! We thought you were dead. I'm afraid that my father (your brother Donald) died ten years ago. We didn't know your address. But we are still living in the same house. Of course you've never met me, but my father often spoke about you. We are very glad you want to come to England. Things have changed in Thetford since you were a girl. Will you be able to come and see us? You will be very welcome.

Very best wishes,
Your nephew,
Oliver

1342 Lone Star Drive
Sweetwater, Texas 77478
U.S.A.
October 17

Dear Ollie,
I can call you Ollie, can't I? I was very sorry to hear about poor Donald. My husband, Hiram, and I will arrive in England on December 12. Will you be able to meet us at the airport? I hope so. Hiram will be too tired to drive after a long flight, and I've never been able to drive.

I enclose a photo of Hiram and me, so you will be able to recognize us. We'll be able to stay with you for two or three weeks. That will be nice, won't it? We can spend Christmas together. Then we'll have to visit Hiram's cousin in Ireland. He wants us to stay with him for a month. We'd like to visit a lot of places in Britain — Buckingham Palace, Oxford, Stratford, Scotland, Wales, and Cornwall. You'll be able to drive us, won't you? We hope to hear from you soon.

With fondest regards,
Auntie Minnie
(Hiram sends his love too.)

P.S. Hiram is on a special diet. He cannot eat meat, fish, fruit, or vegetables.

Exercise

Write a short letter (about 60 words) from Oliver to Aunt Minnie.

🎧 **Listening 1**

Listen to the airport announcements and complete the chart.

FLIGHT DEPARTURES INFORMATION				
AIRLINE	FLIGHT NO.	TIME	DESTINATION	GATE
Global				
British Airways				
AeroMexico				
Japan Airlines				

A: Do I check in here for Global Flight 179 to Caracas?

B: Do you already have your ticket?

A: Yes, I do.

B: Thank you. May I see your passport?

A: There you go.

B: Can you put your luggage up here, please?

A: Sure.

B: Just one case?

A: Yes, that's all.

B: Did you pack the case yourself?

A: Yes, I did.

B: And you haven't left it anywhere, have you?

A: No, it's been with me all the time.

B: Are there any electrical items in the case?

A: No, there aren't.

B: OK. That's fine.

Global/Caracas
British Airways/ London
Japan Airlines/ Tokyo
AeroMexico/ Acapulco
Air Canada/ Vancouver

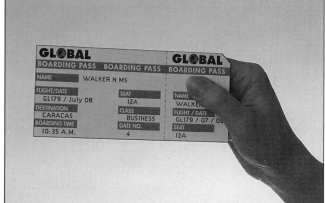

B: Do you have a seating preference?

A: Yes, I do. I'd like a window seat, please.

B: Fine. Seat 12A. Here's your ticket and your boarding pass.

A: Thank you.

B: The flight leaves from Gate 4 in the South terminal. Please report to the gate by 10:30. Enjoy your flight!

C: (Buzz!) Excuse me, ma'am. May I see the contents of your pockets?

A: Of course.

C: Thank you. Put everything in this container. Now please go back and come through the detector again.

A: Sure. (Buzz!) Oh, wait! It's my metal comb…. Here it is.

C: That's fine. Put it with your other things. Now come through again.

window seat
aisle seat
seat with extra leg room

Gate 4/South Terminal/10:30
Gate 36/North Terminal/9:45
Gate 14/East Terminal/11:15
Gate 59/West Terminal/11:00

metal comb
calculator
car keys
house keys

🎧 **Listening 2**

Listen to the in-flight announcement and complete this chart.

FLIGHT NO.	ALTITUDE:	TEMPERATURE:
	SPEED:	TIME OF ARRIVAL:

I've cut myself!

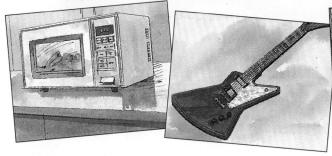

Listen to the five dialogues and match them with the pictures.

A: Ow! This knife's sharp! I've cut myself.
B: Let me see. Oh, you haven't cut yourself badly. It's just a scratch.
A: But it's bleeding!
B: It's not bleeding much. I'll get a Band-Aid.

C: Did you see the play on Channel 13 last night?
D: No, I didn't. What was it?
C: *Romeo and Juliet.* I cried.
D: You cried? Why?
C: Well, it was very sad. At the end, Romeo killed himself, and then Juliet killed herself.
D: It sounds dumb to me. Why did they kill themselves?
C: For love.
D: Oh! They were dumb, weren't they?

E: My guests tonight are the rock stars, M.C. Malone and T.N.T. Katz.
F: Hi, Sid. We're happy to be here.
E: You both play the guitar and sing very well. How did you learn?
F: Well, we just bought some guitars and we taught ourselves.
E: You taught yourselves—terrific!

G: I'm sorry I'm late.
H: Oh, that's all right, Yolanda.
G: Yesterday was my first wedding anniversary.
H: Congratulations!
G: Thanks. We went to that new restaurant on Bank Street.
H: Did you enjoy yourselves?
G: Oh, yes! We had a very good time.

I: Have you seen my new microwave oven?
J: No, I haven't.
I: Oh, it's fabulous. It has an automatic timer. It can turn itself on and off. And it cleans itself!

Exercise

I've cut myself.
1. She's holding a mirror. She's looking at . . . .
2. Be careful, John! Don't hurt . . . .
3. He taught . . . to play the guitar.
4. Romeo and Juliet killed . . . .
5. We went to a party last night. We enjoyed . . . very much.
6. My cassette player is automatic. It turns . . . off.
7. They're enjoying . . . . They're on vacation.

Pet Store Attendant: Hello. How are you today? Can I help you?

Customer: Yes. I'm looking for a pet for my son. Can you suggest anything?

Attendant: What kind of pet does he want? A traditional pet—a cat or a dog? Or something unusual?

Customer: Well, he'd like a snake or an alligator, but he isn't going to get one.

Attendant: We have a nice dog right now—a Rottweiler.

Customer: A Rottweiler! Oh, no! I've heard about them on the news. They're very big and mean.

Attendant: Oh, no, ma'am. They aren't as mean as some dogs.

Customer: Really?

Attendant: Yes, really. Last week we had a small dog here. It was only as big as your purse, but it was as mean as the devil. It bit me three times!

Customer: Let's forget dogs, then.

Attendant: What about a cat?

Customer: A cat. Hmm…. They aren't as friendly as dogs, are they?

Attendant: No, but they don't eat as much as dogs either. And they're very clean.

Customer: Hmm….

Attendant: Or what about a bird? A parrot or a parakeet. We have both.

Customer: Which do you recommend?

Attendant: Well, parakeets aren't as easy to train, and they never speak as well as parrots.

Customer: Yes, but parakeets don't need as much space as parrots, do they?

Attendant: That's true. Parakeets are very popular because they're so easy to keep.

Customer: Yes, but they're a little noisy, aren't they? I want a quiet pet.

Attendant: A quiet pet? Well, what about a goldfish? There's nothing as quiet as a goldfish.

1. Mick/Jack/strong
Mick is as strong as Jack.

2. Her hair/his hair/long
Her hair isn't as long as his hair.

3. work hard/your boss
Do you work as hard as your boss?

4. jumbo jets/Concorde/high
Jumbo jets don't fly as high as Concordes.

5. Tom/drunk/soda/Josh
Tom hasn't drunk as much soda as Josh.
Tom/eaten/pies/Josh
Tom hasn't eaten as many pies as Josh.

Rosalie/Soul/expensive

laptop computers/personal computers/big

drive fast/the world champion

Fred/Dan/hard

the Tigers/scored/points/the Eagles

today/yesterday/wet

English/Chinese/difficult

type carefully/Elizabeth

Marie/Anna/well

Mary/spent/money/Donna

the apartment building/the church/high

my writing/her writing/clear

speak well/the teacher

Sam/Bill/carefully

Ron/caught/fish/Bob

this sack/that sack/heavy

expressways/country roads/interesting

dance beautifully/Anne

Frank/Rockie/loudly

Mr. Jones/bought/food/Mr. Smith

THE DAILY SUN

VOL LVII NO. 20 — **THURSDAY, MAY 5** — **75 CENTS**

$50,000 BANK ROBBERY

LONE ROBBER SHOOTS GUARD IN ESCAPE

NEW YORK, May 4 There was a bank robbery in the downtown financial district today. Just before closing time a man entered the Wall Street branch of First City Bank of New York. He was carrying a shotgun and wearing a nylon stocking over his head. There were only a few customers in the bank at the time. He made them lie on the floor, then forced a teller to put money into a sack. As he was leaving, a security guard tried to ring the alarm. The robber shot him, and the guard is now in St. Joseph's Hospital. Surgeons are trying to save his life. Last night the police arrested a man on Staten Island. The police are interrogating him.

STATEMENT DJ 5573984

Date of birth: 7/24/69　Sex: M

Statement of: John Patrick O'Brien

Residing at: 257 Clark Ave., Richmondtown, Staten Island, NY 10306

Statement taken at: Richmond Police Headquarters　　this 5th day of May

at approximately 09:15 hours in the presence of Angel Rodriguez, Det., NYPD

Detective Sergeant Rodriguez has advised me of my rights under the law and I make this statement freely.

Yesterday afternoon I went to the races at Montvale with my friend, Bobbie Ann Chase. We left my apartment on Staten Island in my black Cadillac and drove to Montvale. We didn't stop for gas, but we got lunch at a fast food place. I don't remember the name of the place, but it was somewhere between Brooklyn and Montvale. We had some hamburgers in the car. We arrived at the racetrack at 12:55 in time for the first race. We stayed there until the last race at 5 o'clock. We were very lucky. I won a lot of money but I can't remember exactly how much. That's why I had a lot of money in my apartment when the police arrived at 6:00. I left Bobbie in midtown Manhattan. She wanted to buy some clothes on Fifth Avenue. I don't know where she is now.

J. P. O'Brien　　　　*Angel Rodriguez Det NYPD*

An interrogation

Fill in the blanks with the correct tag questions.
You're John Patrick O'Brien, *aren't you?*

Police Detective: You're John Patrick O'Brien, . . .?

O'Brien: Yes, I am.

PD: You sell used cars, . . .?

O'B: Yes, I do. And other things.

PD: You live on Staten Island, . . .?

O'B: Yes, I do. I live in Richmondtown.

PD: You went to the races at Montvale yesterday, . . .?

O'B: That's right.

PD: You weren't alone, . . .?

O'B: No, I wasn't. I was with my—friend, Bobbie Ann Chase.

PD: But you're married, . . .O'Brien?

O'B: No. Who told you that?

PD: You left your apartment at eleven o'clock, . . .?

O'B: Yes. About eleven.

PD: You were in your Cadillac, . . .?

O'B: Yes, I was.

PD: You didn't stop for gas, . . .?

O'B: No.

PD: You had lunch at a Chinese restaurant, . . .?

O'B: No, we didn't. We had lunch at a fast food place.

PD: You don't remember the name of the place, . . .?

O'B: No, I'm afraid I don't.

PD: You had fried chicken, . . .?

O'B: No, no. We got some hamburgers to go and ate in the car.

PD: You got to Montvale racetrack in time for the first race, . . .?

O'B: Yes, correct.

PD: You were very lucky, . . .?

O'B: Yes, I really was.

PD: You won $50,000, . . .?

O'B: I can't remember exactly how much.

PD: There was $50,000 in your apartment, . . .?

O'B: Was there?

PD: You don't know where Bobbie Ann is now, . . .?

O'B: No, I'm not her husband, . . .?

PD: But you left her in midtown Manhattan because she wanted to buy some clothes.

O'B: Yes, that's right.

PD: It's interesting, . . .O'Brien? You have a very fast car, . . .?

O'B: What do you mean?

The last race at Montvale started late, and it didn't finish until twenty-five after five, so you drove from Montvale on Long Island to midtown Manhattan to Staten Island in 35 minutes—at rush hour! That's impossible,..., O'Brien?

Jake: Hi, great to see you! Come in.

Kate: Hi, Jake. Uh…I'm not the first, am I?

Jake: No, the others are all in the dining room. The food's in there. Let me take your coat.

Kate: Thanks. Oh, I brought some flowers.

Jake: Thank you. I'll put them in some water right away.

Kate: Is Bruce coming?

Jake: He's already here. Go on in.

in the dining room
by the pool
in the living room
in the backyard

flowers/in some water
candy/on the table
cookies/in the kitchen
cheesecake/in the refrigerator

Amy: Hi, Kate. I like your dress!

Kate: Thanks. Have you seen Bruce ?

Amy: Bruce? Oh, yeah—Bruce. He was here a second ago. Have you had something to eat?

Kate: No, not yet.

Amy: The vegetables and dip are over there, help yourself.

Kate: Thank you.

Amy: There's some salad over here. And there are some potato chips and nuts on the table.

Kate: OK, see you later.

a second ago
a minute ago
a few minutes ago
just now

salad/potato chips
fruit punch/nuts
cheese dip/snacks
ice cream/cookies

Jake: Hello, Kate. Not dancing?

Kate: No, I'm just hanging out. You didn't see Bruce in the kitchen, did you?

Jake: No.

Kate: Oh.

Jake: Hey, this is a great song, isn't it? Do you want to dance?

Kate: Sure, why not?

song
cassette
CD
band
tape

Amy: Well, here's your coat. Thanks for coming.

Kate: It was nice of you to invite me. I really enjoyed myself.

Amy: Good. You've got to come to Jake's birthday party next month.

Kate: OK. What happened to Bruce? Do you know?

Amy: He left early, I think.

Kate: I didn't see Michelle either.

Amy: No, I think she left early too.

Kate: Oh, well, thanks again. Bye.

Jake's birthday party
our Thanksgiving party
our barbecue
my New Year's party

Together Again

Kelly Strong and Rod De Biro are in the studio. They're acting in a scene from *Together Again*. In the movie, Kelly is Constance, a young nurse in Africa. Rod is Armand, a famous zoologist.

Orson: OK, scene thirty-four, take eight. Let's try it again. Action!
Kelly: I love you, Armand.
Rod: I love you, too, Constance. But I have to go…
Kelly: I know *(sob)*, but…perhaps we'll never see each other again!
Rod: We will, Constance, because we love each other!
Orson: Cut! Cut! Cut! That's not good enough. Take five, everybody!

Orson: OK, Kelly. Come over here. Now, I know you don't like Rod, and I know he doesn't like you…
Kelly: Like! We hate each other, you know that.
Orson: But you're actors, and in the movie Constance and Armand love each other, right?
Kelly: Right, but…
Orson: No "buts." You have to look at each other, you have to touch each other, smile at each other, hold each other, and kiss each other. Right?
Kelly: Right, but it's not all my fault. You know Rod, he's selfish. He only thinks about himself, he talks about himself all the time, and he only wants to see himself on film.
Orson: I've heard this before, Kelly. Rod said exactly the same about you!

HOLLYWOOD NEWS MAY 28

SUPERSTAR STRONG QUITS MOVIE!!!

Yesterday, Kelly Strong quit the billion-dollar Megasel movie, *Together Again*. She walked out of the studio after an argument with costar Rod De Biro. "It was impossible," said Ms. Strong, "We just couldn't work together. We weren't enjoying ourselves. We've never liked each other very much anyway. I never want to see de Biro—or Charles Orson—again."

Exercise

He doesn't like her. She doesn't like him.

They don't like each other.

Now you do the same.
1. She has to kiss him. He has to kiss her.
2. I won't see you. You won't see me.
3. He hates her. She hates him.
4. She didn't look at him. He didn't look at her.
5. He hasn't spoken to her. She hasn't spoken to him.

So am I!

A: I'm taking my vacation next month.
B: Really? So am I.
A: I need a change.
B: So do I. I'm tired of the same office and the same people every day!
A: Right! Where are you going?
B: Florida.
A: Oh, really? I went there last year.
B: So did I. We always stay on the Florida Gulf Coast. We never go to Miami or Palm Beach.
A: No, neither do I. It's too crowded there. Where exactly are you going?
B: Sanibel Island. It's about fifty miles south of Sarasota. Do you know it?
A: You're kidding!
B: No, I'm not. I've been there three times.
A: Well, so have we. And we're going there this year too.
B: Not to the Sand Dollar Resort?
A: Yes, why?
B: Well, I'll see you there. That's my hotel too.

🎧 Listening

You are going to hear eight sentences. Listen and check (✓) the response that is true for **you**.

1. ☐ So am I.   ☐ I'm not.
2. ☐ So have I.   ☐ I haven't.
3. ☐ So do I.   ☐ I don't.
4. ☐ So was I.   ☐ I wasn't.
5. ☐ Neither am I.   ☐ I am.
6. ☐ Neither have I.   ☐ I have.
7. ☐ Neither did I.   ☐ I did.
8. ☐ Neither do I.   ☐ I do.

Look at this:

Statement	Agreeing	Disagreeing
I'm tired.	So am I.	I'm not.
I'm not tired.	Neither am I.	I am.
I like music.	So do I.	I don't.
I don't like music.	Neither do I.	I do.
I've heard the news.	So have I.	I haven't.
I haven't heard the news.	Neither have I.	I have.

Exercise 1

Now complete this chart.

Statement	Agreeing	Disagreeing
I was wrong.	So . . .	I . . .
I wasn't right.	Neither . . .	I . . .
I enjoyed the movie.	. . .	. . .
I didn't enjoy the concert!	. . .	. . .
I don't like snakes.	. . .	. . .
I understood the play.	. . .	. . .

Exercise 2

Respond to these statements. Make your responses true for **you**.

LEARNING ENGLISH

I'm not very good at English pronunciation.
I did some homework last night.
I always write down new words.
I never use a dictionary.
I've studied English for a long time.
I understand more than I can say.
I don't like tests.
I translate everything in my head.
I had a dream in English once.
I haven't visited the U.S.A.

A family problem

Vassar College
Poughkeepsie, NY 12601
May 5

Dear Daddy,

Thank you very much for the birthday present. I was very pleased with the Porsche, but I didn't like the color, so I'm going to take it back and change it.

I saw Marc again yesterday. You're worried about him, aren't you? Well, don't worry about him. He's all right. He's very good at his job. He's a drummer in a rock band. I'm going to come to Washington next weekend. I'll bring Marc so you can meet him.

Love,
Caroline.

P.S. We love each other very much. He isn't interested in your money.

From the office of

SENATOR THORNTON J. CALHOUN
THE SENATE
WASHINGTON, D.C.

May 15

Dear Caroline,

I'm sorry about last weekend. I was very upset with Mr. Rodberg (I can't call him "Marc"), but he was very rude to me. I'm <u>not</u> a stupid old fool. I'm tired of dumb young men. I couldn't talk with him about anything.

You love him, I know. I just feel sorry for you, and I'm worried about your future. Your friend likes rock music. He isn't interested in anything else. He isn't interested in you at all. You're making a terrible mistake. And I'm glad he isn't interested in my money, because he isn't going to get any of it!

Love,

Signed for Senator Calhoun in his absence by
Joseph D. Pollard (Secretary to the Senator)

Exercise

I'm interested in politics.
What are you interested in?

I'm good at English, but I'm not very good at math.
What about you?

I'm worried about the environment.
What about you?

I'm tired of this town.
What about you?

I'm very pleased with my English.
What about you?

I'm never rude to people.
What about you?

The Yes/No Contest

Hi there! I'm Barry Smiles. Welcome to the *Yes/No Contest*. Our rules are very simple. I'll ask you questions for thirty seconds. You must answer, but you can't answer with "Yes" or "No." You can't nod or shake your head either. Now, here is our first contestant, Anne Mock from Palm Beach, Florida.

Smiles: What's your name?
Anne: Anne. Anne Mock.
Smiles: Where are you from, Anne?
Anne: Palm Beach.
Smiles: Did you say Palm Springs?
Anne: No, Palm…. *(Gong!)*
Smiles: Oh, I'm sorry, Anne. You said "No." Our next contestant is Chuck Fleener from St.Louis, Missouri. It's *Doctor* Fleener, isn't it?
Chuck: That's right, but call me Chuck.
Smiles: Fine. You aren't nervous, are you, Chuck?
Chuck: I'm not nervous.
Smiles: Did you shake your head?
Chuck: I didn't.
Smiles: Are you sure?
Chuck: Yes, I'm…. *(Gong!)*
Smiles: Oh! I'm sorry, Chuck. Better luck next time. Now, here's our third contestant. He's Richard Oropallo from Washington, D.C. Hello, Richard.
Richard: Hello, Barry.
Smiles: You work in a bank, don't you?
Richard: That's correct.
Smiles: Do you like your job?
Richard: I enjoy it very much.
Smiles: Oh, do you?
Richard: I said, "I enjoy it very much."
Smiles: Now, you aren't married, are you?
Richard: I am married.
Smiles: Is your wife here tonight?
Richard: She's at home in Washington.
Smiles: So she isn't here.
Richard: Of course not.
Smiles: Do you have any children?
Richard: I have two children.
Smiles: Two boys?
Richard: A boy and a girl.
Smiles: And… *(Buzz!)* That's thirty seconds! You've done it, Richard! Isn't that wonderful, everybody? He's won tonight's jackpot prize— a brand-new, fully automatic dishwasher!

Look at these expressions:

Yes	No	?
That's right.	That's wrong.	I don't know
That's correct.	That isn't correct.	I'm not sure.
Of course.	Of course not.	I'm not certain.
That's true.	That isn't true.	
I agree.	I disagree.	

A: Hello, Tom? This is your Dad—your old Dad in the nursing home. Why aren't you here?

B: Oh, hi, Dad. Uh…I'm very busy. I can't visit you today. Uh…I'm sorry, Dad.

A: Tom, Tom! You used to visit me. You used to take me to the movies. You used to bring Barbara and the children.

B: I'm sorry, Dad. We'll come for your birhday.

A: My birthday! It's today! You didn't even send a card. I'm writing a new will!

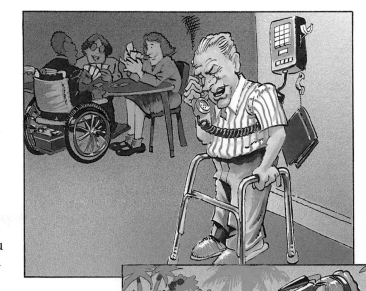

C: Reggie, you used to be the best baseball player in the National League. Are you going to come back and play again?

D: No, I'm not. No way.

C: Why not?

D: Well, baseball used to be the most important thing in my life, but it isn't anymore. I used to practice every day. I never used to go out, or eat big meals or stay up late.

C: Why has your life changed, Reggie?

D: Well, I was poor then, but I'm not now. I don't need to play baseball anymore!

E: Mom?

F: What?

E: There's a terrific movie downtown.

F: Really? What is it?

E: *Spacecop.*

F: Are you going to see it?

E: I'd like to. All the other guys are going, but I don't have any money.

F: OK, OK. How much do you want?

E: Ten dollars.

F: Ten dollars! When I was your age I used to get two dollars for the movies!

E: I know, I know. And you used to walk five miles to school, and you used to cut wood—

F: And I used to talk to my mother with respect!

Exercise 1

I used to eat a lot of candy when I was young, but I don't anymore.
What about you?
What did you use to do when you were young, that you don't do any more?

Make more sentences.

Exercise 2

Talk about your grandparents (and great-grandparents). How was life different for them? What kind of things did they use to do?

A busy office

J.P. Powell: Yes, Erica, what is it?

Erica Mills: Bob Hudson wants to speak with you, J.P.

J.P.: I'm very busy right now. Ask him to call back later.

Erica : All right.

J.P.: Oh, and Erica, tell Chris to fax the sales report to the Toronto office.

Erica: OK. Anything else?

J.P.: Yes. Tell Helen not to call her friends on the office phone.

Erica: All right, I will.

Erica: Hello? This is Mr. Powell's assistant again. I'm afraid Mr. Powell's very busy right now. Could you call back later?

Hudson: All right. Thanks.

Erica: Oh, Chris?

Chris: Yes, Erica?

Erica: J.P. wants you to fax this report to Toronto.

Chris: OK. I'll do it later.

Erica: No, Chris. Do it now. I know it's important.

Erica: Helen, did you call your friend on the office phone yesterday?

Helen: Well…uh…yes. I did. But it was urgent.

Erica: I think J.P. heard you. He wasn't very pleased about it. Don't use the office phone for personal calls, OK?

Helen: Yes. OK, Erica. I won't do it again. I'm sorry.

J.P.: Erica, did you speak with Bob Hudson?

Erica: Yes, I did. I asked him to call back. He says he'll call you later.

J.P.: Fine. Has Chris faxed that report yet?

Erica: Not yet, but I told him to do it immediately. I think he's doing it now.

J.P.: Good. Did you tell Helen not to call her friend from here?

Erica: Yes, I told her not to use the office phone for personal calls. She says she won't do it again. I'm sure she won't.

J.P.: Well, I hope you're right. Her friend is working in Saudi Arabia!

Look at this:

"Ask him to call back later."
"Could you call back later?"
She asked him to call back later.

"Tell her not to use the telephone."
"Please don't use the telephone."
She told her not to use the telephone.

Exercise

"I can't do it." (he says)
He says he can't do it.

1. "That'll be all right." (she thinks)
2. "It's important." (we know)
3. "He's busy." (I'm afraid)
4. "She won't do it again." (she's sure)
5. "She called her boyfriend." (she's sorry)
6. "Her friend is living in Saudi Arabia." (they say)

Latka was a customs officer in Europe. He used to work in a small border town. It wasn't a busy town, and there wasn't much work. The road was usually very quiet, and there weren't many travelers. It wasn't a very interesting job, but Latka liked an easy life. About once a week, he used to meet an old man. His name was Spevna. He always used to arrive at the border early in the morning in a big truck. The truck was always empty. After a while Latka became suspicious. He often used to search the truck, but he never found anything. One day he asked Spevna about his job. Spevna laughed and said, "I'm a smuggler."

Last year Latka moved to the United States. One night he was having dinner in a restaurant in Los Angeles. On the other side of the restaurant he saw Spevna drinking champagne. Latka walked over to him.

Latka: Hello, there!
Spevna: Hi!
Latka: Do you remember me?
Spevna: Sure, of course I do. You're a customs officer.
Latka: I used to be, but I'm not anymore. I retired last year, and I live with my daughter in Los Angeles now. I often used to search your truck in the old country.
Spevna: But you never found anything!
Latka: No, I didn't. Can I ask you something?
Spevna: Of course you can.
Latka: Were you a smuggler?
Spevna: Of course I was.
Latka: But the truck was always empty. What were you smuggling?
Spevna: Trucks!

Interviewer: Good afternoon. Mrs. Archer?

Rita: Yes?

Int: I'm from Channel Five TV. We're doing a survey.

Rita: Oh, really?

Int: Could I ask you a few questions?

Rita: Well, uh…

Int: First, did you watch TV last night?

Rita: Yes, after dinner. From about seven o'clock.

Int: And did you watch any of our programs?

Rita: Yes, most of the evening. Till eleven.

Int: So you saw *Animals in Focus*. What did you think of it?

Rita: It was very interesting. I like wildlife programs.

Int: So you're interested in wildlife?

Rita: Uh-huh. That kind of program always interests me. It's very difficult to film animals, you know.

Int: What about your husband? Did he watch it?

Rita: Only for about five minutes. He's not interested in animals…. Look, I'm very sorry, but I have to pick up the kids from school. Are there many more questions?

Int: Oh, I'm sorry. I'll give you the questionnaire. Could you and your husband complete it and mail it to us?

Rita: Sure.

Exercise

Look at Rick and Rita's comments. Look at the chart.
Complete columns 1 and 2 for Rita and Rick.

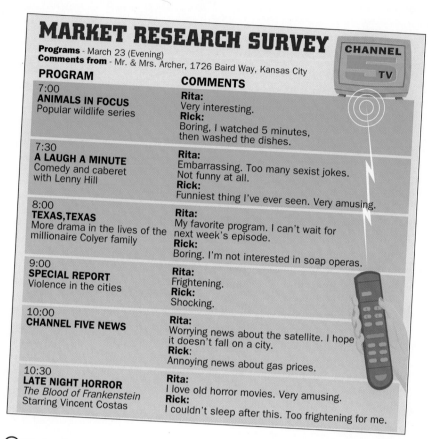

MARKET RESEARCH SURVEY CHANNEL 5 TV

Programs - March 23 (Evening)
Comments from - Mr. & Mrs. Archer, 1726 Baird Way, Kansas City

PROGRAM	COMMENTS
7:00 **ANIMALS IN FOCUS** Popular wildlife series	**Rita:** Very interesting. **Rick:** Boring, I watched 5 minutes, then washed the dishes.
7:30 **A LAUGH A MINUTE** Comedy and caberet with Lenny Hill	**Rita:** Embarrassing. Too many sexist jokes. Not funny at all. **Rick:** Funniest thing I've ever seen. Very amusing.
8:00 **TEXAS, TEXAS** More drama in the lives of the millionaire Colyer family	**Rita:** My favorite program. I can't wait for next week's episode. **Rick:** Boring. I'm not interested in soap operas.
9:00 **SPECIAL REPORT** Violence in the cities	**Rita:** Frightening. **Rick:** Shocking.
10:00 **CHANNEL FIVE NEWS**	**Rita:** Worrying news about the satellite. I hope it doesn't fall on a city. **Rick:** Annoying news about gas prices.
10:30 **LATE NIGHT HORROR** *The Blood of Frankenstein* Starring Vincent Costas	**Rita:** I love old horror movies. Very amusing. **Rick:** I couldn't sleep after this. Too frightening for me.

Listening

Listen to the interview with Mrs. Zimmerman. Complete column 3 for her.

PROGRAM	Rita (1)	Rick (2)	Mrs. Zimmerman (3)
Animals in Focus	She was interested.	He was bored.	She was amused.
A Laugh a Minute			
Texas, Texas			
Special Report			
Channel Five News			
Late Night Horror			

Look at this:

I'm bored.	It's boring.	It bores me.
He's interested.	It's interesting.	It interests him.
She's worried.	It's worrying.	It worries her.
We're frightened.	It's frightening.	It frightens us.
You're amused.	It's amusing.	It amuses you.
They're shocked.	It's shocking.	It shocks them.
I'm embarrassed.	It's embarrassing.	It embarrasses me.
I'm annoyed.	It's annoying.	It annoys me.

Advice

Nick: Hi, Keith. How's it going?
Keith: Oh, hi.
Nick: You don't look very happy. What's up?
Keith: Oh, nothing really. I bought these jeans about two weeks ago, and they're too tight. I have to lose weight.
Nick: Maybe you should go on a diet.
Keith: Sure, but what kind of a diet?
Nick: You should eat lots of salad and fruit.
Keith: I hate salad. I prefer meat, and french fries...and I love candy!
Nick: There you go! You shouldn't eat too much meat, and you shouldn't eat candy at all.
Keith: I know, Nick. Believe me, I know!

✔ salad
✘ red meat
✔ vegetables
✘ candy
✔ mineral water
✘ soda
✔ fish
✘ french fries
✔ fruit
✘ cookies
✔ low-fat yogurt
✘ ice cream
✔ low-fat spread
✘ butter
✔ sweetener
✘ sugar

Yoko: What's the matter, Dario? You're very quiet today.
Dario: I'm worried about my English.
Yoko: What's the problem?
Dario: I'm not practicing enough.
Yoko: Why not?
Dario: Well, it's hard to meet Americans.
Yoko: You should go out more.
Dario: Where should I go?
Yoko: Maybe you should join a gym or take a class.
Dario: Americans never speak to me.
Yoko: Well, you should speak first.
Dario: What can I talk about?
Yoko: Sports! They're always interested in sports!

What's the matter?
What's the problem?
What's up?
What's wrong?

join a gym
take a class
go on a trip

sports
the weather
health
your country

Karen: Hello, Brian. You look tired today.
Brian: Yes, I'm working too hard.
Karen: You should take a few days off.
Brian: I know I should, but we're just too busy. I'm working twelve hours a day.
Karen: Twelve hours a day! You're going to kill yourself!
Brian: What else can I do?
Karen: Maybe you should quit.
Brian: I can't. I need the money.

a few days
some time
a couple of days
a week

12 hours a day
6 days a week
7 days a week
52 weeks a year

Exercise

Make sentences with *should* and *shouldn't*:
1. Your friend wants to lose weight.
2. Someone wants to learn your language.
3. Your friend wants to be a millionaire.
4. Someone wants to meet new friends.
5. Your friend wants to be fitter and healthier.
6. Someone wants to get a raise.

Awards for bravery

Every year *U S News* gives awards for bravery. This year's winners are waiting to collect their awards. Look at the picture, then read the newspaper extracts. Can you guess who the winners are? Find the people in the picture.

The US News Annual Bravery Awards

TWINS SAVE BOY 1
Nine-year-old Darryl Magnusson is the luckiest boy alive! Darryl was playing on a frozen lake when the ice broke and he fell through. Fifteen-year-old twins, Mandy and Marie Fox, heard his cries. Mandy held Marie's feet while Marie lay on the ice and pulled him out.

SHOCK FOR ROBBER 2
A robber got a shock when he tried to rob the store of seventy-eight-year-old Mrs. Flora Dobson. She hit the robber with her walking stick, knocked him out, locked the door of the store, and called the Chicago police.

TRUCK DRIVER HERO 3
Forty-year-old truck driver, Mack Foden, is the hero of the Colorado town of Silver Springs. He was driving down the hill into town when his truck caught fire. The truck was carrying gasoline. Mack drove the truck off a bridge into the river. He is in the Silver Springs Medical Center.

TRAVIS FREE— KIDNAPPERS ARRESTED 4
Travis Barnes, the eighteen-year-old son of billionaire Texas oil man, J.R. Barnes, is free again! He escaped from a house in Lubbock early this morning. Travis climbed out of a window and called 911. The kidnappers were still in bed when the police arrived. Travis's first question to police was, "Will I get the million dollar reward?"

DOG DOES IT AGAIN! 5
Old Shep has done it again. Old Shep, a black and white sheepdog, barked loudly when he smelled smoke at his home in Oxford, Mississippi. Everyone was able to get out before the house burned to the ground. Last year Shep saved the lives of the Faulkner family when their trailer caught fire on Highway 55 outside of town.

MOUNTAIN RESCUE DRAMA 6
Sam and Jasmine Chang saved their father's life after an accident on Overlook Mountain near Woodstock yesterday. David Chang was walking on the mountain with his teenaged children when he fell and knocked himself out. It was snowing heavily, but Sam and Jasmine managed to carry him down the mountain to safety.

Congratulations!

David: I'm David Burns, and I'm going to announce the winners. Senator Cheryl Adams is going to present the awards. And our first winner is 78–year-old Mrs. Flora Dobson. You all remember her. She's a very brave woman! She's the one that knocked out a robber with her walking stick. Step over here, Mrs. Dobson!

Senator: Congratulations, Mrs. Dobson. Is that the stick that knocked him out?

Mrs. Dobson: Pardon me? Oh, yes. This is the one, all right. This is the one that knocked him out. I hit him like this....

Senator: Oh, dear. You won't hit me, will you?

David: Well, thank you, Mrs. Dobson.

Mrs. Dobson: Pardon me?

David: Thank you, thank you. And our second winner is Mr. Mack Foden. He's the one that drove his truck into Silver Creek, and saved a town.

Senator: Congratulations, Mr. Foden. You were very brave. How's your leg?

Mr. Foden: Not too bad now. Thank you, Senator.

David: And now we have a pair of twins. Mandy and Marie Fox from Wisconsin. You all remember them. They're the ones that pulled a nine-year-old boy from a frozen lake last January.

Senator: Well done. Which one of you is Mandy, and which one's Marie?

Mandy: I'm Mandy.

Marie: And I'm Marie.

David: Next we have…

Exercise

Look at this:

1A Two girls saved a boy.

1B Are these the girls?

Yes, they're the girls that saved a boy.

2A A truck went into the river.

2B Is that the truck?

Yes, that's the truck that went into the river.

Continue:

3A A man escaped.

3B Is that the man?

4A A dog saved a family.

4B Is that the dog?

5A Two children carried their father down a mountain.

5B Are those the children?

6A The letters arrived last week.

6B Are those the letters?

Steve: Hi, Amber. Is the boss in?

Amber: Yes, Steve. Ms. Arnold's in her office, and she's waiting for you.

Steve: Oh. Has she been waiting long?

Amber: Yes, she has. She got in at twenty to ten.

Steve: Twenty to ten! So she's been waiting for twenty minutes. Wow! I'm in trouble.

Amber: Well, she isn't very happy.

Alice: Well, Vera Parker. Hello! Are you waiting to see Doctor Lightfoot?

Vera: Hi, Alice. Yes, I am.

Alice: How long have you been waiting?

Vera: Well, let's see. I've been waiting since nine o'clock.

Alice: So you haven't been waiting long. It's only ten after nine.

Vera: Right, I haven't. I've been reading this magazine. There's an interesting article here about operations.

Alice: You shouldn't read that, Vera. You'll be worried.

Vera: No, I won't. I enjoy medical articles, you know. I've been reading about heart surgery. There are some great pictures! Look! Alice…Alice…are you OK?

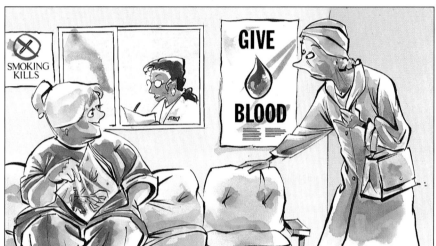

Sally: Dan, call the waiter again!

Dan: I've been trying to call him, Sally.

Sally: But, Dan, we've been sitting here for twenty minutes, and I'm not going to wait any longer.

Dan: I'm sorry, Sally, but he's talking to that woman.

Sally: Yes, I see. He's been talking to her since we came in. Excuse me! Waiter!

Waiter: Yes, ma'am. Do you want your check?

Sally: The check! We haven't seen the menu yet!

Exercise

She's waiting. She arrived five minutes ago.

She's been waiting for five minutes.

They're waiting. They arrived at nine o'clock.

They've been waiting since nine o'clock.

Continue.

1. He's sitting in the chair. He sat down ten minutes ago.

2. They're watching TV. They turned it on at eight o'clock.

3. He's writing a letter. He started fifteen minutes ago.

4. She's listening to the radio. She turned it on at 7:30.

5. They're talking to each other. They met five minutes ago.

6. It's raining. It started an hour ago.

Before you begin

What are the milestones in your life? (The most important things that have happened to you.) Write a list of **five** things.

Ask another student about his/her list.

What kind of things were on your list? Ask and answer these questions.

First day at school

Passed the test for a driver's license

Birth of my daughter

Met Suzanna for the first time

First visit to Europe

Milestones (2)

Make a list of five **other** milestones in your life.

People
When did you meet your best friend?/your partner (husband, wife, boyfriend or girlfriend)?
How long have you known each other?

Education
Do you remember your first day at school? What happened?
What's the best/worst/funniest thing that happened at school?
Have you taken any important exams?
Do you remember your last day at school?

Family
Do you remember a wedding? birth? birthday? Family Party?
What happened?

Vacations
What's the best/worst vacation you've had?
What places have you been to?
What do you remember most about them?

Career
(If you have a job)
Do you remember your first day?
What's the best/worst job you've had to do?
What's the most important thing that has happened to you at work?

Events
Have you been involved in any important events (e.g., wars, earthquakes, hurricanes, accidents)?
When? What happened?

🎧 Listening

Listen to the recording.
Check the things that the woman mentions as milestones in her life.

- ☐ a birth
- ☐ a death
- ☐ a marriage
- ☐ a party
- ☐ a meeting
- ☐ a special place
- ☐ a promotion
- ☐ an accident
- ☐ an embarrassing experience
- ☐ a frightening experience
- ☐ a vacation
- ☐ an interview

A court case

A few months ago, there was a bank robbery in San Francisco. The police arrested a man and a woman. They're in court now. Mrs. Kato saw the robbery. She's on the witness stand. The judge and the twelve members of the jury are listening to her. A lawyer is asking her some questions.

Lawyer: Now, Mrs. Kato. You saw the bank robbery, didn't you?

Mrs. Kato: Yes, I did.

Lawyer: You saw a man, didn't you?

Mrs. Kato: That's right. I saw him when he went into the bank and when he came out.

Lawyer: Now, look around the court. Do you see that man?

Mrs. Kato: Yes. He's the one! He's the man I saw.

Lawyer: He wasn't alone when he went into the bank, was he?

Mrs. Kato: No, he wasn't. He was with a woman.

Lawyer: Now, do you see that woman in the court?

Mrs. Kato: Yes. There! She's the woman I saw.

Lawyer: I see, Mrs. Kato. Now look at the man and woman again. This is very important. Are you absolutely sure about them?

Mrs. Kato: Absolutely sure. They're the people I saw.

Lawyer: Now, Mrs. Kato, what was the man wearing when he went into the bank?

Mrs. Kato: I don't remember everything, but I remember his hat and his bag.

Lawyer: Look at Exhibit A on the table. Is that the hat?

Mrs. Kato: Yes, that's the hat he was wearing.

Lawyer: And Exhibit B?

Mrs. Kato: Yes, that's the bag he was carrying.

Lawyer: Do you remember anything about the woman?

Mrs. Kato: Yes. She was wearing a black wig and red high-heeled shoes.

Lawyer: How do you know she was wearing a wig, Mrs. Kato?

Mrs. Kato: Because it fell off when she was running to the car.

Lawyer: Look at Exhibit C on the table. Is that the wig?

Mrs. Kato: Yes, that's the wig she was wearing.

Lawyer: And Exhibit D. Look at the shoes.

Mrs. Kato: Yes, they're the shoes she was wearing.

Lawyer: Thank you, Mrs. Kato.

Exercise

They're the people.
She saw them.
They're the people she saw.

1. She's the woman. He knew her.
2. Those are the shoes. He was wearing them.
3. That's the house. She's going to buy it.
4. That's the book. She's been reading it.
5. He's the person. I met him.

The empty chair

Jerry Streisen, a friend of mine in Boston, almost had a nervous breakdown last year. I told him to go to a doctor.

Doctor: Hello, Mr. Streisen. What's the problem?
Jerry: I'm very tense and nervous, doctor. I haven't been able to sleep for days.
Doctor: Hmm. Have you been working hard?
Jerry: Yes, I've been working twelve hours a day.
Doctor: Well, you should take a few days off. Go someplace quiet and peaceful, like Nantucket. It's a quiet island near…

Jerry took a boat from New Bedford to Nantucket and arrived late Friday evening. He rang the doorbell of a boarding house, and the owner, Mrs. Searcy, answered the door. Then she showed him to his room. Jerry was very tired and went straight to bed. He slept well and didn't wake up until nine o'clock the next morning.

Jerry went downstairs for breakfast. Because there weren't any other guests, Mrs. Searcy invited him to have breakfast with her and her daughter, Catherine. Catherine was already sitting in the dining room. She was about thirteen years old, with long black hair and clear gray eyes. Mrs. Searcy went to the kitchen to make breakfast. Jerry and Catherine looked at each other nervously for a few seconds.

Jerry: There are four places at the table. Is there another guest?
Catherine: No. We never talk about the empty place.
Jerry: "The empty place?" What do you mean?
Catherine: Well, that used to be my father's place.
Jerry: "Used to be?" I don't understand.
Catherine: My father worked on a fishing boat. Three years ago he went out on his boat, and he never came back.
Jerry: What happened to him?
Catherine: Nobody knows. They searched everywhere, but they never found anything. My mother always keeps that place for him, and she makes his breakfast every morning. That's a picture of him…over there on the wall. My mother's been waiting for him for three years.

Jerry said nothing, but he looked worried. At that moment, Mrs. Searcy came into the room. She poured three cups of coffee and put one cup at the empty place. Jerry looked more worried, and he stared at the empty chair. Suddenly, he heard footsteps outside the door, and a tall man with a black beard walked into the room. It was the man in the picture! Jerry jumped up and ran out of the room.

Man: Who was that? What's the matter with him?
Mrs. Searcy: I don't know. I don't understand. He's a guest from Boston. He arrived last night after you went to sleep.
Man: Catherine, do you know anything about this?
Catherine: No, Daddy, I don't. But he's here because he's very nervous. He says he's hiding here because a tall man with a black beard is trying to kill him.
Man: Catherine, have you been telling stories again?
Catherine: *(laughing)* Stories, Daddy? Me?

Exercise

Mark these sentences true (✓) or false (✗).
1. Jerry went to Nantucket for business.
2. Jerry was the only guest at Mrs. Searcy's.
3. Catherine's father was dead.
4. Her father was the man in the picture.
5. A bearded man was trying to kill Jerry.
6. Catherine was about 30 years old.
7. Catherine has told untrue stories before.
8. Jerry was a very nervous person.

Bank Officer: Please have a seat.
Esther: Thank you. I'm Esther Rosales. I've had an account here for ten years.
Bank Officer: What can I do for you, Ms. Rosales?
Esther: Well, I want to borrow some money.
Bank Officer: What for?
Esther: I want to buy a car… I've been saving for one.
Bank officer: How long have you been saving?
Esther: I've been saving for two years.
Bank Officer: How much have you saved?
Esther: I've saved about $5,000.

Wayne: What are you reading?
Pablo: *The Godfather.* I've never seen the movie, and Bruce told me to read it.
Wayne: It's a very long book! How long have you been reading it?
Pablo: For nearly a month, and I haven't finished it yet!
Wayne: How many pages have you read?
Pablo: About 400. I don't like long books.
Wayne: Neither do I.

Attendant: Yes, ma'am. What can I do for you?
Driver: Hi! Fill it up, please.
Attendant: Regular unleaded or super?
Driver: Regular unleaded. It's nearly empty. I've been driving all day.
Attendant: Oh, really? How far have you driven?
Driver: About 400 miles…from Atlanta.
Attendant: That's a long way. Check the oil?
Driver: Yes, OK.

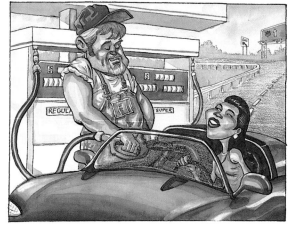

Exercise 1

She/two years/$5,000.
She's been saving for two years.
She's saved $5,000.

Now you do the same:
They/six months/ $1,800.
He/a year/$4,000.
We/three years/ $8,000.

Exercise 2

I/*The Godfather*/a month/400 pages.
I've been reading The Godfather *for a month.*
I've read 400 pages.

Now you do the same:
He/*War and Peace*/a week/250 pages.
She/*Moby Dick*/two weeks/300 pages.
I/*Gone with the Wind*/ ten days/500 pages.

Exercise 3

She/all day/400 miles/Atlanta.
She's been driving all day.
She's driven 400 miles.
She's driven from Atlanta.

Now you do the same:
He/since nine o'clock/ 300 miles/Dallas.
We/for six hours/250 miles/Tampa.
They/since breakfast/ 350 miles/Memphis.

🎧 Listening

Listen to the news report and answer these questions.
1. How long has she been jogging?
2. How far has she traveled?
3. How much money has she collected?
4. How many pairs of running shoes has she used?

Operation Diamond

Andrea Garvey is the Assistant Director of the Department of Customs and Immigration. She is preparing her agents for a special operation.

Good morning, ladies and gentlemen. You were all at Friday's meeting. Are there any questions? No? OK, take out the photographs from your folders. Look at photograph 1. That's Barry Siegel. He's the man that usually flies the diamonds into the U.S.A., and he's the one that will land at the Circle-K Ranch tomorrow night. Be careful, he's very dangerous. He's the one that shot a Federal agent last year.

Now, photograph 2. That's Gulliver. He's the one we really want. He's the one the Mexican police arrested last year, but they had to release him because they couldn't find any diamonds with him. He controls 20% of the illegal diamond trade. He's the one we have to catch with the diamonds and the money.

Look at photograph 3. Look at the woman on the right. Her name's Betty-Lou Harris. She's working for us. She'll be at Gulliver's house at the ranch. She's the one that gave us the information. Watch out for the two men on the left, Farrell and Casey. They're the ones we've been following. They always carry guns, and they're the ones that will shoot first. Ms. Harris is probably the one they'll shoot.

Do you all have photograph 4? Good. Look at the airplane; it's a Cessna 310. It's the airplane that brings in the diamonds. It's the kind of plane that can fly under radar, land anywhere, and take off quickly. You can forget the registration number. It's different every time.

OK. Photograph 5. That's the area they're going to land in. Look at the trees in the background. They're the trees we're going to hide in. There's a road behind the trees, and that's the road they'll have to use. It's the only one.

Finally, photograph 6. The Circle-K Ranch. It's very nice, isn't it? Gulliver has three houses, and this is the one he paid almost five million dollars for last year. Look at the car outside. That's the car that will meet the plane. It's the car he always uses. We want Gulliver, Siegel, the diamonds, and the money all together. Any questions? No? OK, good luck.

Exercise

Look at these examples:
She's the woman. I know her.
She's the woman I know.

He's the man. He met me.
He's the man that met me.

That's the plane. I flew in it.
That's the plane I flew in.

It's the gun. It killed him.
It's the gun that killed him.

Continue:
1. He's the man. He went to Brazil.
2. She's the woman. I met her.
3. They're the shoes. I was wearing them.
4. That's the man. He lives near me.
5. There's the bridge. We crossed it.
6. There's the house. We used to live in it.
7. Those are the packages. They arrived today.
8. That's the woman. She'll be president some day.
9. He's the man. I spoke to him.
10. It's the truck. It crashed.

A: Hello. Lobster Palace Restaurant.
B: I'd like to make a reservation for tonight.
A: All right. What time?
B: Eight o'clock.
A: Eight o'clock. For how many?
B: There are ten of us.
A: Ten! We don't usually take large parties.
B: I know, but we are regular customers.
A: What's your name, please?
B: Diana Ross.
A: Ms. Ross! Of course, that'll be all right. Party of ten at eight.

tonight/8:00/ten
tomorrow night/
    9:30/eight
Saturday evening/
    8:45/seven
next Friday/10:00/
    nine

C: I'd like to get two seats for the concert on Thursday.
D: Where would you like to sit?
C: I'm not sure.
D: Well, here's a seating plan of the concert hall.
C: How much is it in the middle section?
D: $45.
C: $45! That's a little too expensive for us. How much is it in the back?
D: $25.
C: That's fine. What time does the concert start?
D: At eight o'clock.

concert/Thursday/
    8:00
symphony/Friday
    night/8:30
ballet/Saturday
    afternoon/3:00
opera/Monday
    evening/7:30

in the middle $45
in the front $60
on the left $30
on the right $30

E: Do you have any seats left on the Bay Area tour tomorrow?
F: Yes, we do. There are a few seats left.
E: Is that the tour that includes the Sonoma Valley?
F: That's right.
E: How long does the whole tour take?
F: About seven hours.
E: Should I pay you now?
F: If you don't mind.

San Francisco Tours
Bay Area and
    Sonoma Valley
    (7 hours)
Sausalito and Giant
    Redwoods (6
    hours)
Big Sur (9 hours)
San Francisco and
    Berkeley (4
    hours)
Golden Gate Bridge
    and Marin
    County (5 hours)

Exercise

Look at the ads and make conversations in pairs. Student A is trying to make a reservation.

Enter the world of gold rush California.
Costumed stage show with singers, dancers,
and specialty acts. Five-course dinner.
Seatings at 8 PM and 10 PM, Tuesday–Sunday
For reservations, call: (415) 435-0984
Facilities for the disabled

THE SOUND OF
SAN FRANCISCO
WASHINGTON AIRPLANE · SERIOUSLY DECEASED
THE STEVE GRAHAM BAND · JANICE JOCLYN

The Millard Auditorium   **Ticket hotline:**
2400 Fulton Street   **(415) 987-0910**
Tickets from $35 to $65   Information line: 24 hours

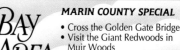

MARIN COUNTY SPECIAL
• Cross the Golden Gate Bridge
• Visit the Giant Redwoods in Muir Woods
• Pt. Reyes National Seashore
• Lunch Included

CALL (415) 567-0213

4-hour tour departs daily 8:30 AM and 1:30 PM
Pick-ups at all major Bay Area hotels

Patti: Jeff, have you seen this ad in *The New York Sentinel?*

Jeff: Yes, I saw it, but I'm not interested in finding a new job. I've been here since I left college. I like working here.

Patti: Really? I've only been here for three years, and I'm already tired of doing the same thing every day. I'm afraid of getting really bored.

Jeff: Oh, come on! It's not that bad. You'll do the same thing there every day.

Patti: Yes, but the salaries are good.

Jeff: I'm not interested in making more money. I have enough now.

Patti: I can never have enough. Of course, you live at home with your parents.

Jeff: I like living with my parents. What's wrong with that?

Patti: Nothing. But I like being independent. I like traveling and I enjoy meeting new people. I'm going to apply for the job.

Jeff: Well, good luck.

JOB OPENINGS

WB WesternBank Inc.

WesternBank Inc. in Tokyo is looking for experienced bank personnel with dynamic personality and minimum 3 years' experience to work in new Japanese branch. Must have Masters in Business Administration. Japanese language instruction available. Positions with more responsibility will open later for the right candidates. Excellent salary with housing allowance.

Write with resume to:
WesternBank Inc., Tokyo 116, Japan

Exercise 1

Answer these questions:
What do you like doing
on weekends?/on vacation?

What do you enjoy doing in the
spring?/summer?/fall?/winter?

Exercise 2

I don't like watching TV.
Write five true sentences.

Exercise 3

flying
He's afraid of flying.

Write sentences using:
going to the dentist
losing his job
dying

Exercise 4

I'm interested in learning English.
I'm not interested in studying history.

Write true sentences.

A: Good morning, Libby.
B: Hi, Jake. It's a nice day, isn't it?
A: Yeah. What are you doing today?
B: I'm not sure. I might go to the beach later.
A: Well, take an umbrella. I've just seen the weather report. It might rain this afternoon.

A: Good afternoon, Mrs. Acuna.
C: Hello, Jake. It isn't very nice today, is it?
A: It was a nice morning. It might stop raining soon.
C: I hope so.
A: Are you playing tennis today?
C: Maybe, it depends on the weather.

A: Good evening, Mr. Pastorius.
D: Good evening, Jake. I think we might have a storm tonight.
A: Oh, really?
D: Yes. The sky's very dark. And I've just heard thunder.
A: Oh, great! I like thunderstorms.
D: I don't. I'm afraid of the lightning.

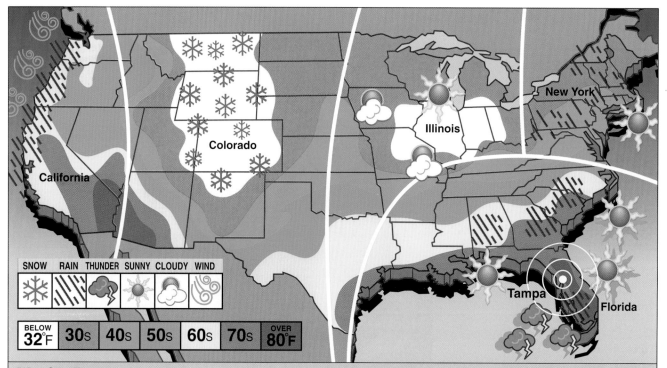

Weather Report
   Good morning, I'm Wayne Porter, and here is the latest weather report from Channel 15. First the national picture. The Pacific Coast will have strong winds which might bring rain from Northern California through coastal regions of the Pacific Northwest. In the Rockies there will be heavy snow. It will be cold and dry in the Midwest, with cloudy skies in the afternoon. Over to the Northeast, where there will be clear skies this morning. There might be some rain in the afternoon, but it won't be heavy. You can expect temperatures in the high 30s to low 40s. Finally, here in the Southeast, it will be warm and sunny in the morning, with a 40% chance of rain in the early afternoon. There will be rain in the evening, and there might be thunderstorms at that time. Now we're going over to Joan Zane in our Tampa studio for your local weather news....

🎧 Listening

Listen to the report for Tuesday, and draw the symbols on the chart.

Pacific Coast	Rockies	Midwest	Northeast	Southeast

Exercise 1

What will the weather be like in California?
It'll be cold and windy. It might rain in the north.

Ask and answer about other areas.

Exercise 2

What will the weather be like here tomorrow?

Waitress: Hurry up, Chef! I have twelve customers, and they all want today's special. Some of them have been waiting for fifteen minutes. They're getting upset.

Chef: I know, I know, but I only have two hands. You'll have to help me.

Waitress: Help you? That's not my job. I'm a waitress, not a cook.

Chef: Well, one of my assistants is off today, and the other is out sick.

Waitress: Oh, OK. What do I do first?

Chef: Well, start putting the meat on the plates, and I'll finish these vegetables.

Waitress: OK. Is that enough meat?

Chef: Hmm. That's a little too much. Take some off.

Waitress: What about potatoes?

Chef: Oh, put on plenty of potatoes, they're cheap—and lots of peas.

Waitress: All right. Can I take them out now?

Chef: Have you put the gravy on yet?

Waitress: Huh? Oh, no, I haven't. Where is it?

Chef: Here it is.

Waitress: Oh, there isn't enough gravy.

Chef: There's plenty in that pot over there.

Waitress: Where? Oh, OK. I've got it.

Chef: Fine. Now you can begin taking the plates out to the customers.

Waitress: Whew! They're hot!

Chef: Well, use a dish towel. And don't carry too many plates. You might drop them.

Waitress: Oh, I won't drop them. I've never dropped a plate in my life! *(Crash!)*

Exercise

Thirty-two people have bought tickets for a city tour.
This is a 40-seat bus.
There are plenty of seats.
This is a 30-seat bus.
There aren't enough seats.

1
Eight people are coming to dinner.
We have 12 water glasses.
We only have seven chairs.

2
This car costs $10,000. Both Helen and Barry want to buy it.
Helen has $12,000.
Barry only has $9,000.

A: Good morning. Can I help you?
B: Yes. I have an appointment with Mrs. Bedoya, the sales manager.
A: What time is your appointment?
B: Eleven-thirty.
A: OK. You're Ms. O'Hare, aren't you?
B: Yes, that's right.
A: Take the elevator to the third floor. Go down the hall to the left. Mrs. Bedoya's office is the third door on the right. You can't miss it.
B: Thank you.
A: Don't bother to knock. Just go right in. She's expecting you.

C: Excuse me.
D: Yes?
C: I'm lost. Is this the way to Disney World?
D: Well, you can get there this way. But it's not the quickest route.
C: Oh, no. Well, can you tell me the best route?
D: Sure. Turn around and go back to the expressway. Turn left and go on until you get to the interstate—that's the I-4.
C: The I-4?
D: That's right. Turn left on the interstate, and follow the signs for Tampa. That's I-4 West. You'll see signs to Disney World after a few miles. It's exit 26.

E: Does this bus go to Fiftieth Street?
F: Yes, it does. Step in, please.
E: What's the fare?
F: A dollar twenty-five.
E: OK. Here's two dollars.
F: Can't you read? "Exact change only."
E: Oh, OK. I have five quarters here. Can you tell me when we get to Fiftieth Street?
F: OK.
E: Thanks a lot.

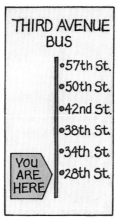

BLOOMBERGER'S

6th FLOOR	Restaurant, CDs, books
5th FLOOR	Furniture
4th FLOOR	China, linens
3rd FLOOR	Men's clothing
2nd FLOOR	Women's clothing
1st FLOOR	Cosmetics, accessories
BASEMENT	Food court, kitchenware

Exercise

Look at the store directory and make conversations. Ask for directions to different sections of the store. You can use some of the expressions below.

Excuse me.
Pardon me.

Can I help you?
May I help you?
Yes, what do you want?

I'm looking for…
I'm trying to find…
Can you tell me where…?
Where's…?
Do you know where (the section) is?

It's on the…
Take the escalator to…
Take the elevator to…
You'll find it on…

Coast Guard rescue

This is the KLLN Radio Newsdesk. It's 5:15. ...A Coast Guard helicopter is trying to rescue a man who has fallen down a cliff in Point Reyes, about fifteen miles north of San Francisco. The man is lying on a small beach at the foot of the cliff. The helicopter has arrived at the scene, and a paramedic has climbed down a ladder to the beach. He's speaking to a doctor on the helicopter by radio.

Paramedic: Hello? Can you hear me, doctor?
Doctor: Yes, I can hear you clearly. Is he unconscious?
Paramedic: No, he's conscious but he looks pretty bad.
Doctor: OK. Ask him if he can move.
Paramedic: Can you move?
Man: No, I...I...
Doctor: Ask him if he's in pain.
Paramedic: Are you in pain?
Man: Oh, yes...I...oh!
Doctor: Ask him where it hurts.
Paramedic: Where does it hurt?
Man: It's...my back.
Doctor: Uh-oh. Don't move him. I'm coming down.

Bob Atkinson is the editor of the *Daily Sun*. He's sending a young reporter, Lois Gold, to interview the singer, Duke Williams.

"Now, I've arranged an interview for four o'clock at his hotel. Ask him lots of questions. You know—ask him if he likes the city. Ask him what his next record will be and when he recorded it, and ask him where. Ask him all the usual questions. But don't...don't ask him how old he is, OK?"

Practice

Now you are the editor. You're sending a reporter to interview some famous people. Tell him or her what questions to ask.
The President of the U.S.A./A famous sports person/A famous actor/A famous singer

Exercise 1

Ask him if he's married.
Are you married?
1. Ask him if he's a student.
2. Ask her if she has a car.
3. Ask him if he can swim.
4. Ask her if she likes coffee.
5. Ask him if he enjoys learning English.
6. Ask her if she got up early this morning.
7. Ask them if they have been to Brazil.

Exercise 2

Is she bored?
I don't know. You ask her if she's bored.
1. Does she have any sisters?
2. Can he drive?
3. Does he speak French?
4. Does she like watching television?
5. Did they go out last night?
6. Has she ever met a movie star?
7. Will they be in class tomorrow?

Exercise 3

Ask her where she lives.
Where do you live?
1. Ask her what time she eats breakfast.
2. Ask her who she met yesterday.
3. Ask her what time she got here.
4. Ask her why she's laughing.
5. Ask her how she gets to work.
6. Ask her how far it is to Miami.
7. Ask her how much money she has.

Exercise 4

Where did he buy his watch?
I don't know. You ask him where he bought his watch.
1. Who did he speak to last night?
2. When did they get married?
3. What has she done today?
4. How many children do they have?
5. Why does he have to go to the police station?
6. How old is she?
7. How much did she pay for her car?

Dick and Janet were driving along a quiet country road in Ohio. They were on their way to Cincinnati. It was almost midnight.

Janet: Dick, look over there. There's something in the sky. What is it?
Dick: I don't know what it is. It's probably a plane.
Janet: I don't think so. It's too big—and too bright.
Dick: You've seen too many movies, Janet. Oh, no!
Janet: What's the matter?
Dick: The engine just died.
Janet: What's happened to it?
Dick: Well, I don't know what happened. We'll have to find a service station.
Janet: There's one in the next town.
Dick: Great, but I don't know if it's open. It's really late.

Suddenly there was a loud noise, and a big, bright silver object flew low over their car. It stopped in midair, turned around, and flew back over their car. Then it went straight up into the sky and disappeared.

Janet: Wow! What was that?
Dick: Huh? Don't ask me. I have no idea what it was.
Janet: Whew! Let's go.
Dick: We can't. The car won't start.
Janet: Try it again.
Dick: That's strange. It's OK now. I wonder why it wasn't working.
Janet: Do you think it was a UFO?
Dick: I don't know. I really don't. We should call the police.
Janet: Do you think they'll believe us?

Exercise 1

Where did it come from? (They don't know)
They don't know where it came from.
1. What was it? (He had no idea)
2. Why wasn't the car working? (They wondered)
3. Where did the object go? (She doesn't know)
4. What will the police say? (They have no idea)

Exercise 2

Was it a UFO? (He has no idea)
He has no idea if it was a UFO.
1. Did it come from another planet? (She wonders)
2. Is the garage open? (He doesn't know)
3. Was it a dream? (We don't know)
4. Will the police believe them? (She has no idea)

THE SAN DIEGO DAILY SUN

VOLUME LXVIII No. 18   **TUESDAY, FEBRUARY 18**   **75 cents**

SUPERTANKER COLLISION DRAMA CONTINUES

SLICK ENDANGERS TOURIST AND FISHING INDUSTRIES

A giant oil slick is threatening marine and bird life and local beaches. Several government agencies are working to prevent the loss of millions of dollars to beach resorts and the fishing industry. Environmental groups say that the government is moving too slowly in the fight to stop pollution.

Yesterday there was a collision about ten miles off the California coast, between the *S.S. Titan*, which is one of the biggest oil tankers in the world, and a Nigerian cargo ship. The collision happened in thick fog late last night and damaged the tanker's engines. It drifted onto rocks and broke in half. The tanker was carrying one million tons of crude oil. The giant oil slick from the tanker is now moving slowly toward the coast around San Diego. Helicopters rescued both crews and nobody died in the collision. Dozens of small boats, which are carrying detergents and straw, are working around the slick.

WHERE'S MY HOUSE

MS. PAT LAINE, WHO LIVES IN Oceanside Cliffs between San Diego and Los Angeles, went home from work last night and couldn't find her house! Ms. Laine's home at 327 Seacrest Drive was near the edge of a cliff, and during the afternoon it fell into the sea. Recent heavy rain has weakened the cliff and more houses might fall into the ocean. Local residents are spending the night in a school, after police warned people not to return to their homes.

SURPRISE FOR A THIEF

SOMEWHERE IN THE SAN DIEGO area a thief is in for a big surprise tonight. Last night someone stole a van which was parked on La Jolla Avenue. The van belonged to the San Diego Zoo. In the back of the van were two boxes which contained poisonous snakes. The van was on its way from the airport to the zoo. The thief took the van while the driver was making a call from a pay phone.

■ WEATHER ■

There will be mostly sunny skies in the San Diego area today. The temperature will be fairly cool, with a high in the mid-50s and westerly winds at 10 to 20 miles per hour. It will be cloudier tonight and the temperature will drop into the low 40s or high 30s. Tomorrow will be cool and cloudy with a 30% chance of rain near the coast and light winds.

■ WORDPLAY ■

How many words can you make? Every word must contain the letter "E". You can use only the nine letters in the grid. You can't use a letter more than once in a word. It's possible to make one 9-letter word.

Score: 20 words or more — excellent
15 words or more — very good
10 words or more — good

A mugging

1

One night Sara Garcia, an elderly widow, was walking down a dark street in Philadelphia. She was carrying her purse in one hand and a shopping bag in the other. There was nobody else on the street except two young men. They were standing in a dark doorway. One of them was very tall with light hair. The other was short and fat with a beard and mustache.

2

The two men waited for a few seconds and then ran quickly and quietly toward Mrs. Garcia. The tall man held her from behind while the other one tried to snatch her purse.

3

Suddenly, Mrs. Garcia threw the tall one over her shoulder. He crashed into the other man, and they both landed on the ground. Without speaking, Mrs. Garcia hit both of them on the head with her purse and walked calmly away.

4

The two surprised young men were still sitting on the ground when Mrs. Garcia crossed the street toward a door with a bright sign above it. Mrs. Garcia paused, turned around, smiled at them, and walked into the Philadelphia Judo Club.

Exercise

Write the story below. The words will help you.

5
Last night, Louis Karpinski/ middle-aged widower/street in Kansas City. He/ briefcase/umbrella. There/ nobody else/two men. They/ alley. One/big/dark hair. The other/thin/bald.

6
They/few seconds and/ walk/slowly/silently/Mr. Karpinski. The big man/ hold/behind. The thin one/ try/steal/Mr. Karpinski/ briefcase.

7
Suddenly, Mr. Karpinski/big one/shoulder. He/collide with/thin one. They/land/ sidewalk. Mr. Karpinski/ hit/umbrella/and/walk/quickly away.

8
The two astonished men sit/ground Mr. Karpinski/ cross/street toward/door/ painted sign. Mr. Karpinski/ stop/turn/laugh/walk into/ Kansas City Karate Club.

Breakfast blues

Mrs. Roth: Adrian! Adrian!

Adrian: What?

Mrs. Roth: Adrian! Come on, it's almost seven o'clock. Your breakfast's getting cold.

Adrian: All right. I'll be downstairs in a minute.

Mrs. Roth: Adrian, you haven't shaved.

Adrian: I know. I'll do it before I go to school.

Mrs. Roth: Well, don't forget. And you need a haircut.

Adrian: All right. I'll make an appointment after I finish school.

Mrs. Roth: And don't forget…write and thank your grandmother for your birthday present….

Adrian: Yeah. I'll do that when I get time.

Mrs. Roth: You'll do it when you get home from school!

Adrian: What about my homework? And I'm going out tonight.

Mrs. Roth: You'll do your assignment and write the letter before you go out. Where are you going anyway?

Adrian: Just out.

Mrs. Roth: Who with?

Adrian: A friend.

Mrs. Roth: Which friend?

Adrian: Just a friend from school.

Mrs. Roth: What's her name?

Adrian: Suzy. She's in my math class.

Mrs. Roth: Well, I'll be out when you get home. You won't go out until your father gets home, will you? He

forgot his keys. He left them on the table.

Adrian: Not again! What time will he be home?

Mrs. Roth: About 7:15. Why?

Adrian: Oh, no! I'm meeting Suzy at 7:30.

Mrs. Roth: Well you'll have to go as soon as he gets home. She'll wait.

Adrian: Will she? You don't know Suzy….

Questions

What'll Adrian do before he goes to school?

What'll Adrian do after he finishes school?

Who'll Adrian write to when he gets time?

When will Adrian do his homework?

When will Adrian be able to go out?

Exercise 1

When/see him/say "Hello."
When I see him, I'll say "Hello."

1. When/see a gas station/buy some gas.
2. After/have breakfast/brush my teeth.
3. As soon as/wake up/get up.
4. Before/go to bed/turn off the light.

Exercise 2

Give true answers:

1. What'll you do when you get home tonight?
2. What'll you do after you have dinner?
3. What'll you do before you go to bed?
4. What'll you do as soon as you get up?

🎧 Listening

Listen to the conversation between Adrian and Suzy.

Check true [✓] or false [✗].

☐ Adrian will leave after his father gets home.

☐ The movie begins at 7:50.

☐ Adrian will be there before the movie begins.

☐ Suzy will wait until 8:00.

Maternity Unit

Mr. Diaz is in the maternity unit. His wife's going to have a baby.

Nurse: Hello. You're Mr. Diaz, aren't you? Have you been waiting long?

Mr. Diaz: Not really. Is there any news?

Nurse: Not yet. We'll tell you as soon as there is. Have you thought of any names for the baby?

Mr. Diaz: Oh, yes. If it's a girl, we'll call her Lucia, and if it's a boy we'll call him Francisco.

Operating Room

David Foster has had a serious accident. His wife's outside the operating room now.

Doctor: Mrs. Foster? I'm Dr. Yamamura.

Mrs. Foster: Oh, doctor, how is he?

Doctor: Well, I'm afraid we'll have to operate.

Mrs. Foster: Oh, no! He's always been afraid of operations.

Doctor: Don't worry. If we operate now, he'll be all right.

Mrs. Foster: Oh, doctor, do you really have to?

Doctor: I'm afraid so. He's lost a lot of blood. If we don't operate, he'll die!

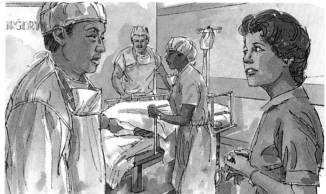

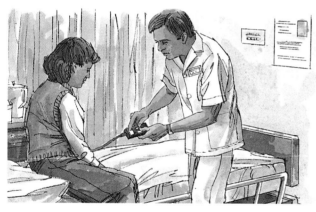

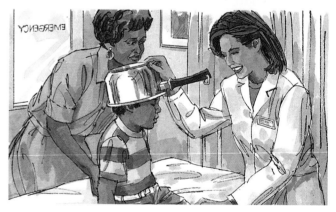

East Wing

Ms. Wright has just arrived at the hospital. She's going to have a minor operation tomorrow.

Nurse: This is your bed, Ms. Wright.

Ms. Wright: Oh, thank you, nurse.

Nurse: Now, get undressed and get into bed. There's a buzzer on the night table. If you press the button, someone will come right away.

Ms. Wright: Oh, I'm sure I won't need anything.

Nurse: Well, don't forget—if you need anything, just press the button.

Emergency Room

Doctor: Oh! How did this happen?

Mother: He was playing soldier, and he put the pot over his head. Now it's stuck!

Doctor: Have you tried to get it off?

Mother: No, I'm afraid of hurting him.

Doctor: Yes, if we pull too hard, we'll hurt him.

Mother: What are you going to do?

Doctor: Well, if I don't get it off, he won't be able to eat!

Mother: Oh, no!

Doctor: I'm only joking. If I put some soap on his head, it'll come off easily.

Exercise

We/operate/he/be all right.
If we operate, he'll be all right.

Write sentences using:
You/take these pills/feel better.
You/eat too much/get sick.
He/press the buzzer/nurse/come.
You/not take the medicine/not feel better.
You/not eat/not get well.
She/have a boy/call/Shawn.

During the next week Melissa received more than 3,000 letters. All of them were asking her for money. Here are three of them.

Million Dollar Winner

Melissa Donahue couldn't believe it when our reporter knocked on her door yesterday morning with a check for a million dollars. She is the first winner in our super million-dollar contest. Melissa is a school bus driver from Detroit, Michigan. We photographed

her outside her home in Detroit. If you want to win a million dollars, turn to page 13 for today's fantastic contest.

VERMONT HISTORIC SOCIETY
Pentonville, Vermont 05151

Dear Ms. Donahue,   April 7

Fort Pentonville was the scene of an important battle during the War of Independence in 1778. It is an important part of our nation's history, and more than 100,000 people visit it every year. Jefferson Hume, in his *Guide to U.S. Battlefields*, said, "Fort Pentonville is the best historic building I have seen."

But Fort Pentonville is in danger. We urgently need money for repairs. If we do not make repairs soon, the roof will fall in, the walls will collapse, and we will lose part of our history forever.

We hope that you will be able to help us.

Yours truly,
Washington T. Adams
Washington T. Adams
Vermont Historic Society

Eureka Apartments
Apartment 429
Kalamazoo, Michigan
49004

April 8

My Dear Ms. Donahue:

Congratulations on your good luck. May I introduce myself? My name is Fredrick T. Boone, M.S. (Linguistics). I have invented a new language, Simplicado. I have been working on it for thirty years. The world needs one language, and English is too difficult. The grammar of Simplicado has only four rules, and the spelling is logical. If people learn Simplicado, everyone will be able to communicate with each other more easily.

I have sent my book, "Simplicado: A World Language" to 139 publishers, and none of them want to publish it. I need $20,000. If I get this money, I will be able to print and market the book myself. If people see the book, they will buy it and I will become rich. I do not want you to give me the money. I want you to lend it to me.

Does this idea interest you? I can come to Detroit and explain my work at any time.

Yours very truly,

J.T.B.

Kyu! (In Simplicado this means "Thank you very much.")

1276 Gateway Road
Kansas City, MO 64108

Dear Ms. Donahue,   April 9

You don't know us. We are sure that you have gotten a lot of letters. We saw your picture in the paper. You look like a kind person, and we need help. We have never written this kind of letter before, but we have tried everything else.

Our baby is very sick, and she needs an operation. There is only one hospital in the world that can do the operation, and it is in Switzerland. We are not rich people. We have been saving for a year, and we have saved $700. But we still don't have enough money. You will help us if you can, won't you? Please.

Yours very truly,
Harriet and Jethro Thomson

Exercise

You are Melissa. Write a reply to one of the letters.

Anne: Lee! You can't park here. There's a fire hydrant.
Lee: Oh, we'll be back in a few minutes. It's OK.
Anne: Oh, no, it isn't. You'll get a parking ticket if you leave it here.
Lee: No, I won't. It's five-thirty. All the traffic cops have gone home.
Anne: Oh, Lee….
Lee: Yes?
Traffic Officer: Is this your car, buddy?

a fire hydrant
a bus stop
a crosswalk
a no-parking sign

Patrol Officer: May I see your license?
Lee: Sure…. Oh, I left it at home.
P.O.: In that case, you'll have to come with us to the station.
Lee: But…but why?
P.O.: You were speeding, buddy.
Lee: But I was only doing thirty-five!
P.O.: There's a thirty-mile-an-hour speed limit. It's a residential section.
Lee: Really? I didn't see the sign.
P.O.: We've been following you.
Lee: So you were doing thirty-five too.
P.O.: No. We were doing sixty miles an hour—and we couldn't catch you!

35 m.p.h./30 m.p.h.
speed limit/
residential section

55 m.p.h./45 m.p.h.
speed limit/
hospital zone

30 m.p.h./25 m.p.h.
speed limit/
school zone

80 m.p.h./55 m.p.h.
speed limit/
federal law

Woman: Hello. Turnpike Service Station.
Lee: Hi. I don't know if you can help me. My car's broken down.
Woman: We have 24-hour service. Where are you?
Lee: I'm on US 31, just south of Hopeville. My car's just past the Lone Star Café. It's a blue Chrysler LeBaron.
Woman: Do you know what's wrong with it?
Lee: I have no idea. But it won't start.
Woman: I'll send a mechanic out to you. She'll be there in about fifteen minutes.

US 31/south/15 min.
I-95/north/half an
hour
Route 66/west/45
min.
Highway 61/east/2
hours

Exercise

The mechanic arrived 15 minutes later.
Use sentences from the boxes,
and make conversations in pairs.

Lee:

Do you know	what's wrong with it?
Do you have any idea	what the problem is?
Can you tell me	

Lee:

| Can you tow me to a service station? |
| Can you fix it? |

Mechanic:

| You've run out of gas. |
| You don't have enough oil. |
| The radiator's empty. |
| The battery's dead. |

Mechanic:

Sure, I'll tow you.	
It's OK, I have	a spare can of gas.
	some oil.
	some water.
	a new battery.

Reservations

Operator: Glory Inn, Atlanta.

Zoot: Hi, this is Zoot Lambert. The manager of Titanium? You know, the band…. I want…

Operator: Please hold, Mr. Lambert. I'm putting you through to the reservations manager.

Zoot: But…

Manager: Mr. Lambert? This is Lauren Perry, the hotel manager.

Zoot: Oh, yeah? Well, I need five rooms for Friday night. That's the 15th. I want the best rooms in the hotel.

Manager: Sorry, I'm afraid I cannot accept your reservation.

Zoot: Now look, we always stay at the Glory Inn…

Manager: I know that, sir. Last time you were here, we had a number of complaints from other guests.

Zoot: You mean they don't like long-haired rock musicians!

Manager: That's not the problem, sir. The band used bad language in the coffee shop, and threw two TV sets into the pool.

Zoot: Yeah, yeah. Well, they'll be more careful this time.

Manager: I'm afraid that's not all, sir. You haven't paid the account for the last time yet.

Zoot: I'll put a check in the mail.

Manager: Please do.

Zoot: So, what about our reservation for Friday?

Manager: I'll answer that very simply, sir. No way!

Zoot asked his secretary to send a letter to the Glory Inn.

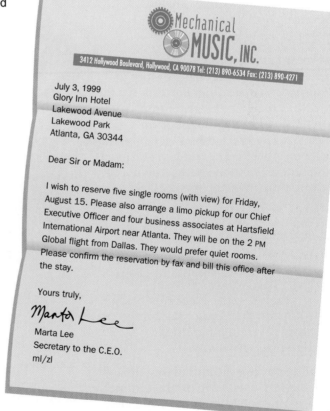

Mechanical MUSIC, INC.

3412 Hollywood Boulevard, Hollywood, CA 90078 Tel: (213) 890-6534 Fax: (213) 890-4271

July 3, 1999
Glory Inn Hotel
Lakewood Avenue
Lakewood Park
Atlanta, GA 30344

Dear Sir or Madam:

I wish to reserve five single rooms (with view) for Friday, August 15. Please also arrange a limo pickup for our Chief Executive Officer and four business associates at Hartsfield International Airport near Atlanta. They will be on the 2 PM Global flight from Dallas. They would prefer quiet rooms. Please confirm the reservation by fax and bill this office after the stay.

Yours truly,

Marta Lee

Marta Lee
Secretary to the C.E.O.
ml/zl

Did Ms. Perry accept the reservation or not? You decide. Write her reply, and lay it out as a formal business letter. You can use some of the expressions in the box below.

Thank you for your letter.
We are pleased to confirm your reservation for…
I'm afraid we cannot confirm your reservation for…
We look forward to seeing you…
I'm afraid we do not want your business.
We hope you will enjoy your stay.
Please call with a credit card number.
We will send the bill to your address.
Please find enclosed a hotel brochure/your last bill…

Exercise

Now write a letter and reserve a room for three nights at the Van der Veld Hotel, 5th Avenue and 61st Street, New York, NY 10021, U.S.A.

59

Operator: Operator 366.
Caller: I've just seen two cars crash into an armored truck. I think it's a robbery.
Operator: Where?
Caller: Just outside the factory gates.
Operator: What factory?
Caller: McManus Forge Company on Old Selma Road.

The first police car got to the factory three minutes later, but it was too late. The robbers had gone. They had knocked out one of the security guards and shot the other. Both guards were lying on the ground near the armored truck. The thieves had taken the payroll for the factory. The police called an ambulance for the guards and questioned three people who had seen the robbery.

Operator: Operator 217.
Caller: I want to report a fire.
Operator: Where is it?
Caller: The Pexico Service Station on Hudson Street. Come quickly!
Operator: Yes. A fire engine will be there in a few minutes.

The fire engine got to the service station just in time. The convenience store in the station was burning. Fortunately the fire hadn't reached the gas pumps and hadn't spread to the neighboring buildings. The fire fighters were able to put it out quickly. The fire had started in the office. Someone had thrown a lit cigarette into a wastepaper basket.

Operator: Operator 577.
Caller: There's a boy in the river. I don't think he can swim. I can see him from my window.
Operator: In the river? Where?
Caller: Oh, I'm sorry. Near Key Bridge. The Washington end of the bridge.
Operator: I'll send a paramedic ambulance right away.

When the paramedic ambulance got there, the boy was lying on the ground. A police officer had seen the boy in the river and had dived in and rescued him. The boy was all right. The police officer had given him artificial respiration. The ambulance took the boy and the police officer to the hospital.

Exercise

3:00: The police arrived. 2:55: The robbers went.
By the time the police arrived, the robbers had gone.

7:00: He got to the airport. 6:50: The plane took off.
• • • .

9:05: The student came to school. 9:00: The class started.
• • • .

4:50: The helicopter arrived. 4:15: The boat sank.
• • • .

11:20: She went out. 11:18: The rain stopped.
• • • .

READERS' LETTERS ----------

Oh, no!…Have you ever had an embarrassing experience? Who hasn't? Last week we asked our readers to tell us about their embarrassing experiences. We received hundreds of letters! Here is a selection.

A SMART TEACHER!

My most embarrassing experience happened when I had just finished college. I had just started teaching at a high school in Denver. One morning my alarm clock didn't go off—I had forgotten to set it. I woke up at 8:00, and school started at 8:30. Quickly I washed, shaved, dressed, jumped in my car, and drove to school. When I got there, classes had already started. I didn't go to the office or the teacher's room but went straight into my first period class. After two or three minutes the students started laughing, and I couldn't understand why. Suddenly, I looked down and understood. I had put on one black shoe and one brown shoe.

Stanley Morris
Boulder, CO

HAND IN HAND

The most embarrassing experience I've ever had happened two years ago. My wife and I had driven into New York to do some shopping. The streets were very crowded, and we were holding hands. Suddenly my wife saw a dress she liked in a store window and stopped. I started looking at some radios in the next window. After a minute or two I reached for my wife's hand. There was a loud scream, and a woman slapped my face. I hadn't taken my wife's hand—I had taken the hand of a complete stranger.

Gary Hall
Paramus, NJ

Why don't you write and tell us about your most embarrassing experience?

My husband and I had decided to buy a new house, and I'd made an appointment to see our bank manager. I'd never met him before, and I was a little nervous. I drove into town, and I was lucky enough to find a parking space outside the bank. I'd just started backing into the space when another car drove into it. I was furious! I opened my window and shouted at the other driver. He ignored me and walked away. It took me 20 minutes to find another space. As soon as I had parked the car, I rushed back to the bank. I was ten minutes late for my appointment. I went to the manager's office, knocked, and walked in. The manager was sitting behind his desk. He was the man who had taken my parking space!

Margaret Larcade
San Antonio, TX

A ghost story

Doug and Kay are staying in an old house on Cape Cod. It belongs to Doug's uncle, and they've borrowed it for the weekend. They arrived an hour or two ago, and they're sitting in front of a fire in the living room downstairs.

Kay: Oh, Doug, this house is fantastic! I love old houses.

Doug: There's a ghost here, you know.

Kay: Doug, don't be silly. Are you trying to scare me?

Doug: No. I've been coming here for years. We used to stay here when I was a kid. I saw the ghost myself once.

Kay: This isn't funny, Doug. And I don't believe in ghosts.

Doug: You don't? Well, I do.

Kay: Where did you see the ghost?

Doug: Upstairs—in the bedroom.

Kay: Yeah, right. Did it have a white sheet over its head?

Doug: No, no. It was just an ordinary ghost. He was wearing clothes from the 1800s.

Kay: He? Who?

Doug: The ghost. I'll tell you about it. I'd been out walking all day and I was really tired, so I went to bed early.

Kay: Had you been reading a book about ghosts?

Doug: No, no.

Kay: Well, go on. What happened?

Doug: I'd been in bed for two or three hours…

Kay: How did you know that it was a few hours?

Doug: There's an old grandfather clock in the bedroom. You'll see it when we go upstairs. Anyway, the ghost was standing beside it.

Kay: What did you do?

Doug: Nothing.

Kay: What did he say?

Doug: Nothing. He just stared at me.

Kay: How did he get into the room? Hadn't you locked the door?

Doug: Yes, I had—and the window too. It was a cold, foggy night like tonight.

Kay: Was there a fireplace?

Doug: Yes, but it was too small for a man to get down. Anyway, there'd been a fire.

Kay: What did you do?

Doug: I sat up and stared back at him. I was too shocked to move.

Kay: Well? What happened?

Doug: I don't know how long we'd been staring at each other, when suddenly I shouted—and he disappeared.

Kay: I don't believe it.

Doug: I didn't believe it myself at the time, but when I told some people who live around here, they believed me. Some of them had seen the ghost themselves. They could even describe him. If you ask them, they'll tell you.

Kay: Doug, put some more wood on the fire. I'm going to sleep right here tonight!

Exercise 1

Choose the correct words to complete the spaces:
Doug (has/had) been walking all day, so he (had been/was) tired. He had (been/be) in bed for a few hours when he (had seen/saw) the ghost. He (had/has) locked the door and window when he (goes/went) to bed, and there had (be/been) a fire in the fireplace. He had been (stared/staring) at the ghost for some time when suddenly he (shouted/had shouted) and the ghost (had disappeared/ disappeared).

Exercise 2

Do you believe in ghosts? Have you ever seen one?
Have you heard any ghost stories? Can you tell one?

In a record store

Liz: Excuse me. I'm trying to find *Rat Run Rap* by *Pleeze B Funky*. It's their latest single.

Salesman: Oh, right. It's number nine this week. CD or cassette?

Liz: CD.

Salesman: It's right here.

Liz: Thanks. And do you have the new album by *Titanium* yet?

Salesman: *Heavy Metal Murder?* Oh, sure. We have that. It's great. You'll love it.

Liz: Oh, it's not for me. It's for my grandmother. It's a birthday present.

THIS WEEK'S TOP TEN HITS

1. Love Me, Baby - Gloria Esterhaze
2. Subway Groove - M.G. Mallet
3. You're My Lady - Jethro P. Crockett
4. The Golden City - Fantasy
5. Happy Summer Days - Danny Kleen
6. Hip Hop Heaven - House 451
7. Blue Jeans Ad Blues - Moaning Wilf
8. Purple Train - Princess
9. Rat Run Rap - Pleeze B Funky
10. The Breakthrough - Streamline Express

In a jewelry store

Ted: I'm trying to find a Christmas present for my wife.

Saleswoman: OK. What kind of thing are you looking for?

Ted: I'm not sure, really. Maybe you can help me.

Saleswoman: How about a bracelet?

Ted: No, I bought her a bracelet for our anniversary.

Saleswoman: Maybe a ring, then. These rings are made of 22-carat gold.

Ted: Mmm. What kind of stone is that?

Saleswoman: A diamond. And it's less than $5,000!

Ted: Oh…. Well, maybe you could show me some earrings, then.

bracelet
pin
chain
ring
necklace
earrings

gold (Au)
silver (Ag)
platinum (Pt)
copper (Cu)

diamond
ruby
emerald
sapphire

In a toy store

Salesman: Do you need any assistance, ma'am?

Mrs. Silva: Thank you. Yes, I'm looking for a toy for my nephew.

Salesman: OK. How old is he?

Mrs. Silva: He'll be nine on Saturday.

Salesman: What about a skateboard?

Mrs. Silva: No, I don't want him to hurt himself.

Salesman: How about a drum set?

Mrs. Silva: I don't think so. His father will be upset if I buy him one of those. Do you have anything educational? You see, he's a very intelligent boy.

Salesman: I have the perfect thing! A do-it-yourself computer kit.

nephew
niece
cousin
aunt
uncle

brother-in-law
sister-in-law
grandfather
grandmother

a toy
present
gift
something

Where is it made?

Carson: Good evening. I'm Jesse Carson, welcome to *Double Your Cash*. Our first contestant tonight is Dawn Sikorski from Lincoln, Nebraska. How are you doing, Dawn?

Dawn: I'm doing fine, Jesse.

Carson: What do you do, Dawn?

Dawn: I'm a librarian.

Carson: And were you born in Lincoln?

Dawn: No, I wasn't. I was born in Omaha.

Carson: OK, now the first question is for $100. Are you ready?

Dawn: Sure.

Carson: Where are Ferrari cars made? Are they made in Spain? Are they made in France? Or are they made in Italy?

Dawn: That's easy. Italy.

Carson: Correct. That's great, Dawn! OK, Dawn, you can take the $100 right now, or you can have another question and double your cash!

Dawn: I'll take another question.

Carson: OK. This is for $200. When was Martin Luther King Jr. murdered? Was it in 1963, 1965, or 1968?

Dawn: He was murdered in…

Here are some more questions in the quiz. Continue the quiz in pairs.
Student A should ask the questions in the blue box; student B should ask the questions in the green box. The answers are at the foot of the page.

$400	Where was Columbus born?	☐ Spain	☐ Italy	☐ Portugal
$800	Where are Boeing airplanes made?	☐ The U.K.	☐ The U.S.A.	☐ France
$1,600	When was uranium discovered?	☐ 1944	☐ 1932	☐ 1789
$3,200	Who was the Statue of Liberty built by?	☐ The French	☐ The British	☐ The Americans
$6,400	Where are space shuttles launched from?	☐ Texas	☐ Tennessee	☐ Florida

$400	Where was John F. Kennedy assassinated?	☐ Dallas	☐ Memphis	☐ Miami
$800	Where are Swatch watches made?	☐ Switzerland	☐ The U.S.A.	☐ France
$1,600	Where is Parmesan cheese produced?	☐ The U.S.A.	☐ Mexico	☐ Italy
$3,200	Which one was born in Arkansas?	☐ Clinton	☐ Bush	☐ Reagan
$6,400	Where was the first book printed?	☐ Britain	☐ Japan	☐ Germany

Exercise 1

Where was your watch made?
Where were your shoes made?
(I think) it was made in Japan.
(I think) they were made in Brazil.

It wasn't made in Germany.
They weren't made in Canada.

| I don't know | where | it was made. |
| I'm not sure | | they were made. |

Ask and answer about your:
pen/pencil/shirt/dress/jacket/jeans/glasses/skirt, etc.

Exercise 2

In your house, is there a television? oven? refrigerator? clock? camera? CD player? vacuum cleaner? hair dryer?
Where was it made?

Exercise 3

What things are made in your country? region? town? capital city?

Exercise 4

The United States imports a lot of things.
Coffee is imported from Colombia.
Cars are imported from Korea.
Make sentences using:
wood/Canada
bananas/Ecuador
beef/Brazil
cameras/Japan
oil/Saudi Arabia

In your country, what goods are imported?
What goods aren't imported?
Where are they imported from?
What things are exported from your country?

Exercise 5

What is produced on farms in your country?
For example:
Bananas are produced in my country.
Rice is produced in my country.

A real bargain

Donna Woo is looking for a new house. She's with the Realtor now.

Realtor: Well, Ms. Woo, this is the house that I told you about: 341 Sunlake Drive. The owners are away, but I have the keys.

Donna: When was it built?

Realtor: It was built in 1936.

Donna: Who built it?

Realtor: I have no idea. Is it important?

Donna: No, I guess not. Is that a new roof? It looks new.

Realtor: It's pretty new. It was put on two years ago.

Realtor: It's in very good condition. The previous owner was a builder.

Donna: I'm worried about the electrical wiring. Has it been rewired?

Realtor: Yes, it has.

Donna: Oh? When was that done?

Realtor: Five years ago. It's been completely renovated. New central heating and air conditioning have been put in, and a new garage has been built.

Donna: Oh? When was that done?

Realtor: The garage? Last year—I think. It's a very solid house. It's built of brick with a tiled roof.

Donna: I have a little boy in elementary school. Does a school bus pass by here?

Realtor: Yes, right here on Sunlake Drive. The children are picked up at eight o'clock, and they're brought home by 3:30.

Donna: It's really not expensive. I've seen a lot of similar houses, and they're more expensive.

Realtor: Oh, yes. It's a real bargain.

Donna: Are there any plans for new construction in this area?

Realtor: Excuse me? New construction? Well, uh, yes, a new hospital is going to be built about six blocks north of here.

Donna: Anything else?

Realtor: Well, a new interstate highway will be built next year. You'll be able to get to the city in half the time.

Donna: Where exactly will the interstate be built?

Realtor: Uh…it'll be built just down the street. Sunlake Drive has been chosen as the main exit for the city. It'll be interesting. You'll be able to watch the traffic….

Exercise

826 Adams Street
Row house
Built: 1925
Wood/shingle roof
Central heating: 1969
Renovated: 1992

826 Adams Street is a row house. It was built in 1925. It's made of wood with a shingle roof. Central heating was put in in 1969 and it was renovated in 1992.

Now write paragraphs about:
2857 Colonial Drive

Ranch-style house
Built: 1971
Brick/shingle roof
Central air conditioning: 1983
Garage converted into room: 1993

648 West 68th Street

Town house
Built: 1895
Brownstone/flat roof
Renovated: 1953
Sauna: 1990

The Six O'Clock Report

Good evening, this is Rose Anne Silvernail with the Six O'Clock Report from WBTV Baltimore.

Our top story tonight: Alan Wolfe, the great plane robber, has been caught in Costa Rica. He was arrested in a San José nightclub. He is being questioned at local police headquarters, and he will probably be sent back here to Baltimore. In 1992, Wolfe was sentenced to forty years in prison for his part in the Great Plane Robbery at Baltimore-Washington International Airport. He escaped from the Maryland State Penitentiary in April. Since then he has been seen in ten different countries.

Another tragedy in the music world: Jerry Henderson, the lead guitarist of the rock group *The Rats*, is dead. He was found unconscious in his room at the Baltimore Glory Inn early this morning. Henderson was rushed to the Johns Hopkins University Hospital but doctors were unable to save his life. A number of bottles, which had been found in his room, were taken away by the police.

The painting *Iris Morning* by Penoir was stolen last night from the Baltimore Museum of Art. The painting, which is worth over five million dollars, had been given to the museum in 1993. It hasn't been found yet, and all area airports, highways, and train stations are being watched. All vans and trucks are being searched. A reward of $50,000 has been offered for information.

And finally, Jumbo, the elephant that escaped from the Baltimore Zoo this afternoon, has been caught. Jumbo was chased across Druid Hills Park and was finally captured at a hot dog stand near the park's main gate. Jumbo had not been fed and was trying to take bread rolls from the stand. A tranquilizer gun was used, and Jumbo was loaded onto a truck and was taken back to the zoo. At the zoo, he was examined by the zoo veterinarian. Fortunately, no damage had been done, and Jumbo will be returned to the elephant house tomorrow.

Look at this:

Someone did it.	*We don't know who did it.* or *It isn't important who did it.* or *We aren't interested in who did it.*	It was done.

(or *We are more interested in **what** was done than in **who** did it.*)

Someone does it....	It is done.
Someone is doing it....	It is being done.
Someone has done it....	It has been done.
Someone had done it....	It had been done.
Someone will do it....	It will be done.

Exercise 1

Someone stole them. *They were stolen.*
Someone has found it.
Someone is watching it.
Someone cleans the windows.
Someone had taken them.
Someone will buy it.
Someone brought it.
Someone has seen it.
Someone is searching them.
Someone had caught it.
Someone will send it.

Exercise 2

Now write the news for today.

TELEVISION

THE CONDOR PASSES
Directed by **Paula Simon** (PBC)

This documentary, which was first shown at the Cartagena Film Festival, will be aired on Wednesday at 8 on PBC. The condor is now found in only a few remote places in the Andes and the Rockies. In recent years, nests have been robbed and eggs have been stolen. Condors are protected by law, but they are threatened with extinction. Paula Simon spent a year making this documentary. The everyday habits of the condor have been recorded for future generations.

BOOKS

ATLANTIC CROSSING
written by **Tyrone Fitzpatrick**
Published by Ransom House, $29.95

This book tells the story of Tyrone Fitzpatrick who crossed the Atlantic Ocean alone in a small wooden boat. The boat was built in Ireland and was designed like the boats that were used by the Irish 1,000 years ago. Fitzpatrick thinks North America was visited by Europeans many years before Columbus was born. The design for the boat was taken from an old book which had been found in an Irish monastery. The book is beautifully illustrated with many color photographs and maps. The photographs were taken by Fitzpatrick himself during the voyage.

REVIEWS

MUSIC

SONGS OF THE CITY
By **Tracy Chaplin** (Somy Music)
Produced by **Carmine Dragone**

All the songs on this new CD were written by Tracy herself, and were recorded live during her recent concert tour. She is accompanied by an all-star group: Melissa Hayes (bass), Ahmed Touré (drums), Zach Zebedee (keyboards), and Bruce Stringbean (guitar). There is a great variety of music on the album — from romantic ballads to sizzling soul. The lyrics are printed in the liner copy.

MOVIES

UFO II (PG)
Directed by **Stephen Spielman**
Written by **Pritchard Rice**
Music composed by **John Williamson**

UFO II, which is now being shown at theaters in major cities, is one of the most exciting movies I've ever seen. It was filmed in Hollywood last year, but the special effects were done at Crittendon Studios in England. Richard Deere is brilliant as the Army general, but the real stars are the UFOs themselves. It can be seen at neighborhood theaters beginning next week. Don't miss it!

∩ Listening

Listen to the radio review and complete the sentences.

1. *Space Opera* was … by Tim Webber.
2. The music was … by the Idaho Symphony Orchestra.
3. The hero is … by Danny Kleen.
4. *Starlight Tonight* is … by Lorna Winter.
5. The costumes were … by Annette Field.
6. The book is … by Appletree Books.

Exercise

Now write a short review of:
a movie that you've seen.
a book that you've read.
a record that you've heard.
a TV program that you've seen.

When Elvis Presley died on August 16, 1977, radio and television programs all over the world were interrupted to give the news of his death. President Carter said: "Elvis Presley changed the face of American popular culture…. He was unique and irreplaceable." Eighty thousand people attended his funeral, and Elvis Presley movies were shown on television and his records were played on the radio all day. In the year after his death, 100 million Presley albums were sold.

Elvis Presley was born on January 8, 1935, in Tupelo, Mississippi. His twin brother died at birth. His parents were very poor and Elvis never had music lessons, but Elvis regularly sang at church services. In 1948, when he was thirteen, his family moved to Memphis, Tennessee. Elvis left school in 1953 and got a job as a truck driver.

In the summer of 1953 Elvis paid four dollars and recorded two songs for his mother's birthday at Sun Records' studio. Sam Phillips, the owner, heard Elvis and asked him to record *That's All Right* in July 1954. Twenty thousand copies were sold, mainly in and around Memphis. Elvis made five more records for Sun, and in July 1955 he met Colonel Tom Parker, who became his manager. Parker sold Elvis's contract to RCA Records. Elvis immediately bought a pink Cadillac for his mother. In January 1956, Elvis recorded *Heartbreak Hotel,* and a million copies were sold. In the next fourteen months he made another fourteen records, and they were all big hits. In 1956 he also made his first movie in Hollywood, *Love Me Tender.*

In March 1958, Elvis had to join the army. When his hair was cut, thousands of women cried. He spent the next two years in Germany, where he met Priscilla Beaulieu, who became his wife eight years later, in 1967. In 1960, he left the army and went to Hollywood where he made several movies during the next few years. Most critics thought the movies were a waste of his talent.

By 1968, many people had become tired of Elvis. He hadn't performed live since 1960. But then he recorded a new album, *From Elvis in Memphis,* and appeared in a TV special. He became popular again, and went to Las Vegas, where he was paid $750,000 for four weeks. In 1972, Priscilla left him, and they were divorced in October 1973. The next few years were spent doing concert tours. Elvis died at home of a heart attack. He had been eating and drinking too much for several years. He left all his money to his only daughter, Lisa Marie Presley.

Since his death, Elvis has sold more records than during his lifetime. He has become a legendary figure, and every year there are rumors that he is still alive. In 1993, Elvis was the first rock musician to be featured on a U.S. postage stamp. People were asked to vote—did they want a picture of the young 1956 Elvis or of the Elvis of the Las Vegas shows. You can see how they voted!

Andy

I have $6,000. I'm going to look at the car. If I like it, I'll buy it.

How much is the car?
Does he have enough money?
Is he going to look at the car?
Will he buy it?
What will he do if he likes it?

Chris

I've worked for an oil company for ten years. I have a B.S. in engineering. I have the qualifications. I'm going to apply for the job. If they offer me the job, I'll definitely take it.

Does he have experience?
Does he have a B.S.?
Is he going to apply for the job?
What will he do if they offer him the job?

Floyd

I'm a mechanic, and I know a lot about cars. I have a current driver's license and enough money. If they ask me, I'll go with them.

What's his job?
How much does he know about cars?
Does he have a current driver's license?
Does he have enough money?
What'll he do if they ask him to go with them?

Jessica

I am a native speaker of English. I can read and write Spanish. I'll apply for the job. If I get it, I'll have to move to New Jersey.

What languages can she read and write?
What languages does she need?
Will she apply?
What'll she have to do if she gets the job?

Darlene

I'm 19 and I'm interested in the job. I'll get more information if I call. If the salary's good, I'll apply.

How old is she?
Is she too old?
What'll happen if she calls?
Will she apply?

FOR SALE: Ford Mustang. Original owner. Very good condition. $6,000. Call 201-684-6073 after 5.

WANTED: Chemical Engineer. Important off-shore oil company. Qualifications: Bachelor of Science and five years' experience in similar work. Send resume to Box 305, New Orleans, LA 70113.

Personal: Two members needed for overland sub-arctic expedition from Burlington, Vermont, to Nome, Alaska, by Winnebago Camper. Applicants must have current driver's license, knowledge of mechanics, and minimum $4,000 for expenses. Write Dick York, Box 96A, Winooski, VT 05679.

WANTED: Bilingual secretary for office in New Jersey. The applicant must be a native speaker of English and must be able to read and write Spanish. Send resume to Texxo Corp. Personnel Department, Princeton, NJ 08540.

WANTED: Beginning computer programmer. Opportunity to learn and work. Applicants must be over 18. For more information call (212) 417-0204 from 9 to 5 weekdays.

Barbara

That's a nice car, but I don't have enough money. If I had enough money, I'd buy it!

Does she like the car?
Does she have enough money?
Will she buy the car? Why not?
What would she do if she had enough money?

Dave

I like that job, but I can't apply for it. I don't have the qualifications. If I had the qualifications, I'd apply for it.

Does he like the job?
Can he apply?
Why not?
What would he do if he had the qualifications?

Tom

I have $4,000 and a current driver's license. But I know very little about cars. If I knew something about cars, I'd go with them.

Does he have a driver's license?
What about money?
How much does he know about cars?
What would he do if he knew enough about cars?

Helen

I am a native speaker of English, but I can't read or write Spanish. If I could read and write Spanish, I would apply for the job.

Can she read and write Spanish?
Does she need Spanish?
Can she apply? Why not?
What would she do if she could read and write Spanish?

Jack

I'm interested in the job, but I'm too young. I'm only 17. If I were older, I'd apply.

Is he over 18 or under 18?
Is he going to apply?
Why not?
What would he do if he were older?

If	I	had enough money,	I	'd	buy that car.
	you	were rich,	you	would	travel.
	we		we		
	they		they		
	she		she		
	he		he		

Bob: Are you hungry?

Liz: Yeah. I didn't have much for breakfast.

Bob: Do you feel like a hamburger?

Liz: OK, I'll have a Big Greg— but no fries for me.

Bob: Anything to drink?

Liz: You've been here before. What are the shakes like?

Bob: Not bad. I'm getting one.

Liz: OK, I'll have a strawberry shake.

Bob: Anything else?

Liz: No, that's all.

Listening 1

Listen to Bob and the counterperson. Circle the items that they ordered on the menu.

GREG BURGER 2 oz burger	$1.95	FRIES	regular large	$0.95 $1.50
BIG GREG 2 x 2 oz burgers	$2.90	COLA	regular large	$1.25 $1.75
QUARTER POUNDER 1 x 4 oz burger	$3.15	SHAKES chocolate, strawberry		$2.50
CHEESE GREG 2 oz burger + cheese	$2.45	COFFEE		$1.25
BEAN BURGER vegetarian burger	$3.00	Our burgers are made from 100% American beef. All our packaging is recyclable.		

Erin: What are you having?

Tina: I don't know. I can't decide.

Erin: I'd have the special if I were you. I had it last time I was here. It was great.

Tina: No, it's got ham on it. I don't like ham. I'll just have the plain pizza.

Erin: A regular or a large?

Tina: Mmmm…a large, I think.

Erin: Are you very hungry?

Tina: No, not very.

Erin: Then I wouldn't have a large one if I were you. They're enormous.

Tina: What about an appetizer?

Erin: OK. Let's have another look at the menu…

Listening 2

Listen to Tina and the waiter. Circle the items that they ordered on the menu.

PIZZA PALACE

PLAIN mozzarella cheese, tomato, onion	$5.95 regular	$7.95 large
HAWAIIAN mozzarella cheese, tomato, onion, ham, pineapple	$6.95 regular	$9.95 large
MARINA mozzarella cheese, tomato, onion, tuna, anchovies, shrimp	$7.95 regular	$10.95 large
PIZZA PALACE SPECIAL mozzarella cheese, tomato, onion, ham, mushroom, peppers	$7.95 regular	$10.95 large

APPETIZERS

Minestrone soup $3.50   House salad $2.50

DESSERTS

Ice cream $2.95   Chocolate mousse $3.50

Listening 3

Listen to Dan and the counterperson. Circle the items that they ordered on the menu.

Dan: What time is it, Roy?

Roy: Twenty after one.

Dan: We don't have much time. Where do you want to eat? Pizza Palace? MacGregors?

Roy: A pizza would be OK if we had more time, but we don't. And I don't really feel like a burger….

Dan: Why don't we just grab a sandwich?

Roy: OK. There's a deli just around the corner.

Dan: Fine. Let's try it.

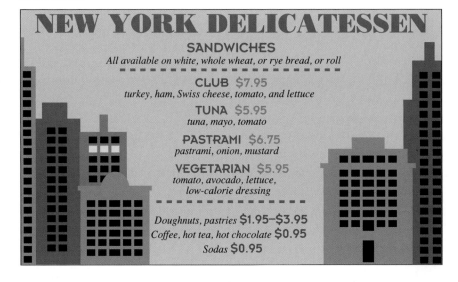

NEW YORK DELICATESSEN

SANDWICHES

All available on white, whole wheat, or rye bread, or roll

CLUB $7.95
turkey, ham, Swiss cheese, tomato, and lettuce

TUNA $5.95
tuna, mayo, tomato

PASTRAMI $6.75
pastrami, onion, mustard

VEGETARIAN $5.95
tomato, avocado, lettuce, low-calorie dressing

Doughnuts, pastries $1.95–$3.95
Coffee, hot tea, hot chocolate $0.95
Sodas $0.95

Offshore oil

On tonight's edition of *Mississippi Magazine* we'll look at offshore oil in the Gulf of Mexico. Oil was first discovered in the Gulf of Mexico in the 1930s. Since then more oil has been found off the coasts of Florida, Alabama, Mississippi, Louisiana, and Texas. More money is being brought into the state of Mississippi from offshore drilling leases. We aren't going to become very rich, but we must decide how to spend the revenue from oil. We took our TV cameras into the streets to ask people their opinion. Our question was: "If you were the governor of Mississippi, what would you do with the money?"

"Well, of course I'm not the governor, but if I were, I'd spend the money on more hospitals and schools. We need more doctors, nurses, and teachers. We don't have enough good teachers. If salaries were higher, we could keep better teachers. And there aren't enough doctors and nurses either because the medical schools are too small. If they were bigger, we would have more doctors and nurses. Money that is spent now on education and health is an investment for the future."

"I think the answer is simple. Taxes are too high in this country. I would reduce state taxes. If we reduce taxes, people would have more money. If they had more money, they'd spend more. Industry would have to produce more, so it would need more workers. There would be more jobs, and we would all be richer."

"I'm very worried about the economy. There aren't enough jobs for everyone, and people with jobs aren't making enough money. If I were governor, I'd help low-income families pay their heating and electric bills. I'd encourage farmers to produce more food, more cheaply. I'd bring more industry into the state. If we did that, everybody would benefit, wouldn't they? There's one thing that makes me happy. I'm glad the money stays in Mississippi. The federal government would spend it on more tanks and bombs."

"There's too much crime and violence nowadays. There aren't enough police officers on the streets. I'd give cities money to increase the size of their police forces, and I'd raise their salaries. If we had more police officers, we'd all feel safer. And I'd increase the benefits for senior citizens. I've worked hard all my life, and I should have a reasonable standard of living."

Exercise

If you were governor of your state/president/prime minister of your country, what would you do?
Why?

What would you do?

Imagine that you are going to a desert island. You can take six things. What six things would you take? Why?

If you weren't here, where would you like to be? Why?

If you could be somebody else, who would you like to be? Why?

If you had a million dollars, what would you do? Why?

If I were you...

I have a headache. *If I were you, I'd* | *take an aspirin.*
go for a walk.
take a nap, etc.

I want to buy a pet. If you were me, what kind of pet would you buy? Why?
I also want to buy a radio/a car/a watch/a camera/an English book.
Give me some advice.

Now advise these people:

I've lost my passport.

I've been bitten by a snake.

I can't sleep at night.

I want to win an Olympic medal.

I cut myself.

I've just seen an accident.

I need some money, and the banks are closed.

I want to get a new job.

I want to be a millionaire.

I've been mugged.

I don't know what to wear...

I'm going to a wedding, and I don't know what to wear!
I'm going to a funeral/a club/a football game/a
picnic/Honolulu/the North Pole/a lecture/the moon.
Give me some advice.

I don't know what to get...

It's my mother's birthday tomorrow, and I don't know what to
    get her.
It's my father's birthday next week. He'll be 47.
It's my brother's birthday next month. He'll be 16.
It's my sister's birthday on Thursday. She'll be 21.
It's my baby brother's birthday tomorrow. He'll be 3.
It's my little sister's birthday on Sunday. She'll be 10.
Give me some advice.

What would you do? What wouldn't you do?

Exercise 1

Complete these sentences from the cartoon:
- ☐ Nothing ... be done.
- ☐ You ... be killed.
- ☐ Pictures from the planet's surface are ... received now, Captain.
- ☐ The planet ... be destroyed.
- ☐ I ... be beaten.
- ☐ You ... to be entertained.
- ☐ They ... be stopped.

Exercise 2

Number the sentences in Exercise 1 from 1 to 7.

Look at this:

Someone will do it...	It will be done.
No one will do it...	It won't be done.
Someone must do it...	It must be done.
No one can do it...	It cannot be done.
Someone can do it...	It can be done.
No one could do it...	It couldn't be done.
Someone might do it...	It might be done.
Someone should do it...	It should be done.
Someone is doing it...	It is being done.
Someone was doing it...	It was being done.

Exercise 3

Complete these sentences with words from below. There might be more than one possible answer to some of them.

should/must/can/might/cannot/must not/should not
1. Elephants ... be found in Africa and India.
2. Pockets ... be emptied before clothes are put into a washing machine.
3. Passports ... be shown when you enter the United States.
4. Life in outer space ... be discovered soon.
5. Personal computers ... be used when planes are taking off.
6. Small children ... be left at home alone.
7. The planet Venus ... be seen without a telescope.
8. Whales ... be killed for food.
9. Dogs ... be left in parked cars on hot days.
10. You shouldn't play with matches. You ... get burned.

Exercise 4

Discuss your partner's answers to Exercise 3.

Reports

Lynn Willis is a new reporter for the *Los Angeles Daily Echo.* Last week several famous people arrived at L.A. International Airport, and Lynn was sent to interview them. Nobody told her very much.

Cristina del Castillo

Secretary General of the United Nations: "I'm very busy. I have a lot of appointments. I can't say very much. I'm happy to be in Los Angeles. I enjoyed my visit in January. I'll be here for only twelve hours. I'm going to meet the governor. I have no other comments."

Lynn's Report

Cristina del Castillo visited California yesterday. She arrived at 10 AM, and we asked her to comment on the international situation. She just made a brief statement. She said that she was very busy and that she had a lot of appointments. She said she couldn't say very much, but she said that she was happy to be here and that she had enjoyed her visit in January. She said she would be here for only twelve hours and that she was going to meet the governor. She said she had no other comments.

Ivan Nystat

European movie director: "I like newspaper reporters, but I don't have time to say much. Just that I'm working at Global Studios in Hollywood. I haven't worked in Hollywood before. I've heard bad things about Hollywood movies in the past, but I can work with the people at Global. It's the best studio in the world, and I'm the greatest director in the world. My new movie will cost eighty million dollars."

Lynn's Report

Academy Award winner Ivan Nystat arrived in L.A. yesterday. Ivan was in a hurry. He said he liked newspaper reporters but that he didn't have time to say much. He said that he was working at Global Studios in Hollywood. Ivan said that he hadn't worked in Hollywood before and that he had heard bad things about Hollywood movies in the past. He said that he could work with the people at Global. He said that it was the best studio in the world, and that he was the greatest director. He also said that his new movie would cost eighty million dollars.

Look at this:

Maria said, "It's my car."	She said it was her car.
Ray said, "I like San Francisco."	He said he liked San Francisco.
Anna said, "I can swim."	She said she could swim.
Lee said, "I thought about you."	He said he had thought about me.
Sue said, "I've been to Paris"	She said she had been to Paris.
Carlos said, "I bought it in Miami."	He said he had bought it in Miami.
Yoko said, "I'll go to L.A."	She said she would go to L.A.

Exercise

Now write reports on these statements, which were also made to Lynn Willis at L.A. International.

Tracy Chaplin, popular singer
"I'm not staying in L.A. long."
"I'm on my way to New Orleans."
"I'm going to record another album."
"I've written ten new songs."
"I like recording in New Orleans."
"I made my last album there."
"I'll be in New Orleans for six weeks."

Reggie Walker, ex-baseball star
"I don't like reporters."
"They've written a lot of lies about me."
"They destroyed my marriage."
"I have a new career."
"I'm tired of baseball."
"I'll never play baseball again."
"I can't say any more."

Oral exams

Stefan: Hey, Marta! Have you finished the exam?
Marta: Yes, I have. Whew!
Stefan: Was it hard?
Marta: Well, yes. It was…pretty hard.
Stefan: Did you pass?
Marta: I don't know. Ms. Nadler didn't tell me.
Stefan: What questions did she ask?
Marta: First she asked me what my name was.
Stefan: That was pretty easy, wasn't it?
Marta: Yes, except I couldn't remember! Then she asked me where I came from and how long I'd been studying here at the institute.
Stefan: And what else did she ask?
Marta: She asked when I had begun taking English, and she asked how I would use English in the future.
Stefan: Yes, yes, go on.
Marta: Then she asked me if I liked the institute and if I lived with my parents.
Stefan: Anything else?
Marta: I'm trying to remember, Stefan. Oh, yes! She asked if I spoke any other languages.
Stefan: Is that all?
Marta: Let's see. Well, she asked me what my hobbies were, and she asked me to tell her about them. Then she gave me a picture and asked me to describe it. Then I was asked to read a passage out loud.
Stefan: What did she say at the end?
Marta: Oh, yes! She asked me to tell you to go in—right away.

This is the list of questions that Ms. Nadler used when she was asking the questions.

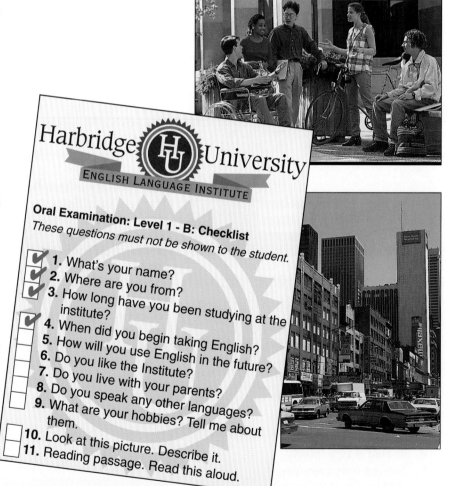

Harbridge University
ENGLISH LANGUAGE INSTITUTE

Oral Examination: Level 1 - B: Checklist
These questions must not be shown to the student.

- ✔ 1. What's your name?
- ✔ 2. Where are you from?
- ✔ 3. How long have you been studying at the institute?
- ✔ 4. When did you begin taking English?
- 5. How will you use English in the future?
- 6. Do you like the Institute?
- 7. Do you live with your parents?
- 8. Do you speak any other languages?
- 9. What are your hobbies? Tell me about them.
- 10. Look at this picture. Describe it.
- 11. Reading passage. Read this aloud.

Look at this:

"Do you like Japanese food?"	(She) asked (him) if (he) liked Japanese food.
"Have you been to Mexico City?"	(He) asked (me) if (I) had been to Mexico City.
"Will you go there?"	(They) asked (us) if (we) would go there.
"What's your address?"	(I) asked (them) what (their) address was.
"How did you come to school?"	(You) asked (her) how (she) had come to school.
"When can you do it?"	(She) asked (me) when (I) could do it.

Travel Agent: Hello. Can I help you?

Marion: I'm interested in your St. Cuthbert vacation package.

Agent: Oh, yes! The Caribbean! I can recommend it highly.

Marion: Can you tell me a little more about it?

Agent: Of course. It's a terrific package tour. You'll travel on a regularly scheduled flight. You'll be met at the airport and taken to your hotel. The hotel has a swimming pool and a great nightclub. It's a very modern resort—it was built last year. The restaurant is wonderful, and you can walk to the beach in two minutes.

Marion: It sounds great! I'd like to make a reservation.

Agent: Just a minute, and I'll get the form to fill out.

KEEP OUT

Marion made the reservation and paid a deposit. Two months later she was in St. Cuthbert. But she was disappointed. When she got home to Chicago, she went to see the travel agent.

Travel Agent: Hello again. Did you have a good trip?

Marion: No, I certainly did not have a good trip!

Agent: Oh, I'm sorry to hear that. What was wrong?

Marion: Well, when I got to St. Cuthbert, I had to spend four hours at the airport. You said we would be met, but we weren't. You also said we would be taken to the hotel. We weren't, and the taxi cost $50!

Agent: I see. You had a very bad start. But the hotel was nice, wasn't it?

Marion: No, it was not! You said it was modern. You were so right. They hadn't finished building it! We couldn't sleep because the construction workers were working all night— on our balcony! You said it had a swimming pool, and it did. But it was empty. And the restaurant! They served canned tuna fish every night—tuna and rice, tuna salad, tuna and spaghetti….

Agent: Oh, no!

Marion: You said that the hotel was near the beach. You said we could walk there in two minutes.

Agent: Couldn't you?

Marion: Sure, but there was one problem. There was an oil refinery between the hotel and the beach, and it took half an hour to walk around it.

Agent: Oh, no! I'm really sorry. We didn't know. We really can't give you a refund, but we can give you a ten percent discount on your next vacation.

Marion: Next vacation! I'm spending my next vacation right here in Chicago!

Come to sunny
MANDANGA

10 Good reasons to stay at the
SAFARI RESORT

1. You'll enjoy the scenery.
2. You'll love the food.
3. The weather is excellent.
4. The staff is very friendly.
5. There are tours every day.
6. You'll be met at the airport.
7. The hotel has three restaurants.
8. You can go horseback riding.
9. You can see the beach from the hotel.
10. Every room has a hot tub.

Exercise

This is an ad for another vacation package tour. Lynn went there.
None of the things the agent said were true.
You said the hotel had three restaurants, but it didn't.
You said we would love the food, but we didn't.
Write down her other complaints to the travel agent.

A: I'm sorry I'm late. I couldn't get the car started this morning.

B: Winter's almost here. The engine was probably cold.

A: It needs a complete tune-up, but garages are so expensive nowadays.

B: Can't you do it yourself?

A: Who? Me? I don't know anything about cars.

B: Well, if I were you, I'd have it done soon. The garage that I use is very reasonable. And have the radiator filled with antifreeze. They say it's going to be a cold winter.

radiator/filled with
   antifreeze
brakes/tested
battery/checked
oil/changed
tires/checked

C: Hi! Do you do alterations?

D: Yes, we do. What do you want done?

C: I'd like to have this skirt lengthened. It's too short for me.

D: Fine. It'll take about two weeks.

C: And at the same time I want to have this dress shortened. It's a little too long.

D: OK. Would you mind putting on the skirt first? You can change in there.

two weeks
three days
a week
ten days

skirt/dress
pants/jeans
jacket/coat
overcoat/raincoat

E: Hello. Can I make an appointment to see the optometrist?

F: Sure. Would next Friday be OK? At three o'clock?

E: Do you have an earlier appointment?

F: No, I'm sorry. That's the earliest.

E: Well, that'll be OK, then. I want to have my eyes tested. I think I need new glasses. Bye.

F: Bye. Oh, be careful. That isn't the door. It's a window.

E: What? Oh, yes, it is a window. Do you see my problem?

optometrist/eyes
   tested
doctor/blood
   pressure taken
dentist/a cavity filled
dentist/my teeth
   cleaned

Exercise

A: I'm driving across the desert next week.
B: You should have your car checked./You should have your radiator checked./You should get it tuned up.

Work with a partner. Give advice in these situations:
My jacket's very dirty.
There are holes in my shoes.
My camera's broken.
My overcoat's too long.
My pants are too short.
I can't see very well.
I have a cavity.
My watch battery is dead.
I often ask people to repeat themselves. I don't hear very well.

Picture 1

Michelle went to the supermarket last Saturday. While she was shopping she met her neighbor, David. David was with his three-year-old son, Joshua.

Make a dialogue from this report of the conversation.
- David asked her how she was.
- She said that she was fine, and asked how Joshua was.
- He told her that Joshua had had a cold.
- She asked if Joshua was better.
- He said that Joshua was fine.

Picture 2

While they were talking, Joshua got bored. He began playing with some jars of coffee. He took a jar from the shelf. It was very heavy. He put the jar into Michelle's shopping bag. She didn't notice.

Make a dialogue from this report of the conversation.
- David said that they were going to meet his wife, Crystal, when she finished work.
- Michelle asked David to give Crystal her best wishes.
- David said that he would.
- David asked Joshua what he was doing.
- Joshua said that he wasn't doing anything.
- David told him not to touch the coffee jars.
- Michelle said good-bye.

Picture 3

As Michelle was leaving the supermarket, a store detective stopped her. She took the jar of coffee from Michelle's bag.

Make a dialogue from this report of the conversation.
- The detective asked her if she had paid for the coffee.
- Michelle said that she never buys coffee.
- The detective asked her why the coffee was in her bag.
- Michelle said that she hadn't known it was there.
- The detective said that she didn't believe Michelle, and asked her to come to the manager's office.

Picture 4

The manager was very angry. There had been a lot of trouble with shoplifters recently.

Make a dialogue from this report of the conversation.
- The manager said that he would call the police.
- Michelle asked him not to.
- She said she hadn't stolen the coffee.
- He said she hadn't paid for it.
- She said it wasn't hers, but offered to pay for it.
- He said that he had to call the police.

🎧 Listening

Listen to what happened next.
Mark these sentences true [✓] or false [✗].

☐ Michelle couldn't guess what had happened.
☐ She thought David had put the coffee in her bag.
☐ The manager believed Michelle's story.
☐ David came into the office.
☐ He couldn't explain either.
What would you do if you were the manager?

The appointment

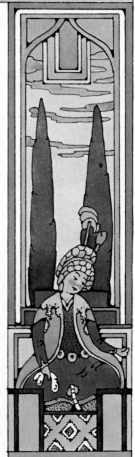

Once upon a time, there was a rich caliph in Baghdad. He was very famous because he was wise and kind. One morning he sent his servant, Abdul, to the market to buy some fruit. As Abdul was walking through the market, he suddenly felt very cold. He knew that somebody was behind him. He turned around and saw a tall man, dressed in black. He couldn't see the man's face, only his eyes. The man was staring at him, and Abdul began to shiver. "Who are you? What do you want?" Abdul asked. The man in black didn't reply.
"What's your name?" Abdul asked nervously.
"I...am...Death," the stranger replied coldly and turned away.

Abdul dropped his basket and ran all the way back to the caliph's house. He rushed into the caliph's room.
"Excuse me, master. I have to leave Baghdad immediately," Abdul said.
"But why? What's happened?" the caliph asked.
"I just met Death in the market," Abdul replied.
"Are you sure?" asked the caliph.
"Yes, I'm sure. He was dressed in black, and he stared at me. I'm going to my father's house in Samarra. If I go at once, I'll be there before sunset."
The caliph could see that Abdul was terrified and gave him permission to go to Samarra.

The caliph was puzzled. He was fond of Abdul, and he was angry because Abdul had been badly frightened by the stranger in the market. He decided to go to the market and investigate. When he found the man in black, he spoke to him angrily.
"Why did you frighten my servant?"
"Who is your servant?" the stranger replied.
"His name is Abdul," answered the caliph.
"I didn't want to frighten him. I was just surprised to see him in Baghdad."
"Why were you surprised?" the caliph asked.
"I was surprised because I have an appointment with him—tonight—in Samarra!"

Exercise

"Excuse me, master. I have to leave Baghdad immediately," Abdul said.
Abdul said that he had to leave Baghdad immediately.

Now change the three conversations into reported speech.

Hopes and plans

Sierra Lindsey, newlywed

Arne Lingstrom, waiter

Amanda Cheng, elementary school student

Kyle Stockard, college student

Barbara Connolly, bank executive

Ahmet Hussein, tennis player

Six people were asked about their hopes and plans. Match what they said to the pictures above. Write the numbers next to the letters.

1.
I want to be the President of the U.S.A., and I want to be real rich, and I want to be on TV…oh, yeah, and I want an ice cream.

2.
I hope we can get an apartment of our own soon—we're living with my parents. We're saving hard and I hope we'll have enough money soon. And of course, we hope to start a family soon. I'd like to have a girl and a boy.

3.
Well, I plan to be a champion. I'm very ambitious. I've been professional for six months. I'm working hard and I intend to get better and better. Also, I hope to make a lot of money. I'm 18 now. I'll have to retire when I'm 35 or 36. I hope I won't have to get a job then!

4.
I just don't know what I want to do. I don't have any plans. You know, you can't plan too far ahead. Something will happen, I guess. You know what they say, tomorrow is the first day of the rest of your life. A big house and a fancy car just don't matter to me.

5.
Plans? Yes, I have made very careful plans. I retire next year. I'm going to sell my apartment in Manhattan, and I'm going to live in Florida. I love golf, and I hope I'll play every day. I'm looking forward to it.

6.
I'm only working here temporarily. I want to work in the movies. I work out every day, and I'm very fit. I'm in better shape than Schwarzenegger or Stallone. If I get the chance, I'll be a movie star. That's my ambition, and I'm going to do it.

Look at this:

| What | are you going
are you planning
would you like
do you want
do you intend
do you hope | to do? |

Talk about your future

Work with a partner and discuss your plans and hopes.
Ask each other these questions:
Do you like what you're doing now?
Do you want to do something different?
What would you like to do?
Would you like to live somewhere else?
Have you made any plans?
Do you intend to continue studying English?
Will you use your English in the future?
What do you hope to do in the future?
What is your greatest ambition?

Vocabulary

This index contains all the words in the Student Book,
and the numbers of the pages where they first occur.

Honolulu 2
hope (n) 80
hope (v) 57
horn 20
horror 37
horseback
  riding 76
hospital 28
hospital zone 58
hot 3
hot chocolate 3
hot dog stand 66
hot tub 76
hotel 8
hotel room 8
hotline 46
hour 8
house 39
house salad 70
housing 47
Houston 64
how 1
huh 52
hundreds 61
hungry 70
hurricane 41
hurry (n) 7
hurry up 13
hurt (adj) 4
hurt (v) 51
husband 28

I
I 1
ice 1
ice cream 29
ID 18
idea 52
identical 3
identification 18
I'd like 1
if 2
ignore 61
illegal 45
Illinois 48
illustrate 67
immediately 35
immigration 45
import (v) 64
import (n) 21
important 2
impossible 28
in 1
in a hurry 7
include 46
incorporated 1
increase (v) 71
incredible 19
independent 47
India 73
industry 53
information 22

information
  desk 8
in front of 6
initial 1
inquiries 2
insert (v) 3
in shape 80
instant 53
in time 28
institute 75
instruction 3
intelligent 12
intend 80
interest (v) 57
interested in 32
interesting 6
interfere 73
international 17
interrogate 28
interrupt 68
interstate 65
interview (v) 6
interviewer 7
into 3
introduce 57
invent 57
investigate 79
investment 71
invite 29
Ireland 24
Irish 67
irreplaceable 68
is 1
island 23
it 1
Italy 64
item 25
itinerary 1
itself 26

J
jacket 64
jackpot 33
Jamaica 1
January 68
Japan 4
Japanese 53
jar (n) 78
javelin 4
jeans 38
jewelry store 63
job 6
jog (v) 44
join 15
joke (v) 56
joke (n) 6
judge (n) 4
judo 54
July 19
jumbo jet 27
jump (v) 4
jumper 4
jury 42
just 2

K
Kalamazoo 57
Kansas City 54
karate 54
keep (v) 27
key 25
Key West 19
keyboards 67
kid (n) 62
kid (v) 31
kid sister 8
kidnapper 39
kids 6
kill 26
kilometer 19
kind 41
kiss (v) 30
kit 63
kitchen 8
kitchenware 50
knife (n) 26
knock (v) 50
knock out (v) 39
know 2
knowledge 69
Korea 18

L
ladder 12
ladies 50
lake 39
land (v) 4
language 53
laptop computer
  27
large 9
Las Vegas 68
last 1
late 5
later 5
latest 48
Latin America 1
latrine 15
laugh (v) 36
launch (v) 64
laundromat 3
lava 23
law 28
lawyer 42
lead guitarist 66
leading (adj) 3
learn 10
lease (n) 71
leather 11
leave 6
lecture (n) 72
left 15
leg 25
legendary 68
lemon 2
lend 57
lengthen 77
less 63
lesson 16
let go 73

let's 3
let's see 2
letter 5
lettuce 70
librarian 64
library 7
license 58
lie (n) 74
lie (v) 28
life 6
lifetime 68
lift (v) 4
light (adj) 53
light (n) 20
lightning 48
like 1
limit (n) 58
limo 59
Lincoln 64
line 2
linens 50
liner copy 67
linguistics 57
list (n) 41
listen 6
Lithuania 4
little 72
live (adj) 4
live (v) 1
living room 29
load (v) 3
local 48
location 1
lock (v) 21
logical 57
London 8
lone 28
long (adj) 7
long (adv) 5
Long Island 28
long jump (n) 4
long-haired 59
look (v) 8
look for 7
look forward
  to 80
Los Angeles 21
lose 38
loss 53
lost 17
lot 1
loud 11
loudly 10
Louisiana 71
love (n) 26
love (v) 13
low 48
low-calorie 70
low-income 71
Lowell 22
Lubbock 39
luckily 4
lucky 6
luggage 25
luggage cart 13

lunch 6
lyrics 67

M
m.p.h. (miles
  per hour) 58
ma'am 8
machine 3
magazine 40
mail (n) 6
mail room 17
mainly 68
major 16
make 3
mall 16
man 4
manage 13
manager 11
Mandanga 76
Manhattan 28
many 1
map 7
march 15
Marin County
  46
marine (adj) 53
market (n) 79
market (v) 57
market research
  37
marketing 2
marriage 41
marry 13
Martinique 1
Mars 72
Massachusetts
  22
master's degree
  17
Masters 47
match (v) 80
matches 73
maternity 56
math 32
matter (n) 5
May 28
may 2
maybe 48
mayo 70
me 6
meal 34
mean (adj) 27
mean (v) 7
measure 3
meat 38
mechanic 58
medal 4
medical 40
medical center
  39
medical school
  71
medicine 56
meet 1
meeting 41

member 42
Memphis 44
men's room 50
mention (v) 41
menu 70
message 2
metal 25
meter 4
metropolitan 16
Mexico 22
Mexico City 75
Miami 1
Michigan 57
microwave
  oven 26
midair 52
middle 1
middle-aged 54
midnight 52
midtown 28
Midwest 48
mile 7
mile(s)-an-
  hour 58
milestone 41
milk (n) 3
million 39
millionaire 38
mine 11
mineral water 9
minestrone 70
minimum 47
Minneapolis 2
minor (adj) 56
minute 3
mirror 8
miss 50
mission 73
Mississippi 8
Missouri 33
mistake (n) 32
mixture 12
modern 76
mom 5
moment 2
monastery 67
Monday 1
money 6
Monterey 7
Montgomery 1
month 6
Montreal 1
moon (n) 72
more 20
morning 4
most 1
mother 10
motorboat 7
mountain 39
mouth 8
mouthwash 9
move (v) 16
movie 30
movie director
  74

ready 3
real 10
really 1
Realtor 65
reasonable 71
recent 53
recommend 27
record (n) 2
record (v) 74
record store 63
recording
  studio 10
recruit 15
recyclable 70
reduce 71
reference 22
refrigerator 29
refund (n) 76
region 48
registration 45
regular 44
regularly 68
regulations 73
remember 8
reminisce 46
remote 67
renovate 65
repairs (n) 57
repeat (v) 77
reply (n) 59
reply (v) 12
report (n) 7
report (v) 25
reporter 4
representative 22
require 2
rescue 8
reservation 19
reserve (v) 59
reside 28
resident 53
residential 58
resort (n) 53
respect 34
responsibility 47
restaurant 26
result 4
resume (n) 47
retire 80
retired 7
return 12
revenue 71
reward (n) 39
rewire 65
rice 64
rich 13
Richmondtown
  28
right (correct) 2
right away 10
right here 5
rights 28
ring (n) 63
ring (v) 23

river 39
road 20
rob 39
robber 28
robbery 60
robe 23
rock (n) 13
rock band 32
rock group 66
rock musician 59
rock star 26
Rockies 48
roll (n) 9
romantic 67
roof 23
room 8
rose (n) 11
Rottweiler 27
route 50
routine 4
row house 65
ruby 63
rude 32
rule (n) 33
rumor 68
run (v) 42
run out (of gas)
  58
running high
  jump 4
running shoes 44
rush (v) 23
rush hour 28
Russian 4
rye 70

S
sack (n) 28
sad 26
safe (adj) 71
safety 39
sail 1
salad 70
salary 69
sales 2
sales
  representative
  22
salesman 63
saleswoman 63
Samarra 79
same 6
Samoa 7
San Antonio 3
San Diego 53
San Francisco 2
San Jose 66
sandwich 70
sapphire 63
satellite 4
Saturday 1
sauna 65
say 5
scare (v) 62

scene 30
scenery 76
schedule 76
school 6
school bus 65
score (n) 4
Scotland 24
scream (v) 23
scream (n) 61
screen (n) 6
sea 7
search (v) 66
seat 11
Seattle 8
second (time) 4
second 50
secretary 22
secretary-
  general 74
see 3
select 3
selection 3
selfish 30
self-teaching 53
senate 32
senator 32
senior citizen 71
sentence (v) 66
Seoul 18
series 37
servant 79
serve (v) 46
service 2
session 10
set (v) 61
seventh 1
several 7
sexist 37
shake (n) 70
shake (v) 8
shampoo (n) 9
shaving cream 9
she 4
sheepdog 39
sheet 62
shelf 78
shingle 65
ship 1
shirt 64
shiver (v) 79
shop (v) 78
shoplifter 78
shopping (n) 61
shopping bag 78
short 8
shorten 77
shortly 2
shotgun 28
should 9
shout (v) 61
show (v) 63
shower (n) 1
shrimp 70
sign (n) 50

sign (v) 15
signature 1
silence 75
silk 11
silly 62
similar 65
sing 10
singer 46
single (n) 63
sir 11
sister 8
sister-in-law 63
sit down 8
situation 74
six 4
sixty 13
sixty-five 16
size 18
sizzling 67
skateboard 63
skirt (n) 64
sky 48
skyscraper 23
slap (v) 61
sleep (n) 8
sleep (v) 8
sleeping pill 8
sleepwalk 8
slick (n) 53
slip (v) 4
slot 3
slowly 12
small 7
smart 13
smell (v) 11
smile (v) 21
smoke (n) 8
smuggler 36
snack (n) 29
snake 27
snatch 54
sneaker 11
snow (n) 48
snow (v) 39
so 1
soap (n) 9
soap opera 37
sob 30
society 57
soda 5
soft 3
soldier 15
solid 65
some 1
somebody 1
someday 45
someone 2
someplace 43
something 5
sometimes 20
somewhere 10
son 7
song 67

Sonoma Valley
  46
soon 5
sore throat 9
sorry 1
soul 67
sound (n) 46
sound (v) 11
the South 1
South America
  17
South Pacific 23
Southeast 48
space 27
spaceship 12
space shuttle 64
space suit 12
spaghetti 76
Spain 64
Spanish 17
spare (adj) 58
speak 2
special (adj) 41
special (n) 70
special effects 67
specialty 46
specialty act 46
speed (n) 24
speed (v) 58
speed limit 58
spell (v) 2
spelling 57
spend 8
spirit 46
sports 38
spray (n) 9
spread (v) 60
spring (n) 47
staff 76
stage show 46
stairs 23
stale 11
stamp (n) 18
stand (n) 66
stand up 15
standard of
  living 71
star (n) 7
star (v) 30
stare (v) 62
starship 73
state (n) 71
state tax 71
statement 28
Staten Island 28
station (n) 58
Statue of Liberty
  64
stay (n) 59
stay (v) 2
St. Cuthbert 76
steal 54
step (n) 53
step (v) 12

stereo 11
stick (n) 39
stick (v) 56
still 24
St. Louis 2
stocking 28
stomachache 9
stone (n) 63
stop (v) 3
store (n) 18
store detective
  78
store window 61
storm (n) 48
storm shelter 23
story 43
straight 15
strange 12
stranger (n) 61
Stratford 24
straw 53
strawberry 70
street 71
streetcar 16
stretch limo 10
strong 8
stuck 12
student 18
studio 7
study (v) 17
stupid 6
subarctic 69
suddenly 8
Suez Canal 19
sugar 3
suggest 27
suitcase 13
summer 21
sun 7
Sunday 1
sunset 79
super 44
supermarket 78
superstar 10
supertanker 53
sure 3
surface (n) 12
surgeon 28
surgery 40
surprise 53
survey (n) 16
survive 23
suspicious 36
sweetener 38
Sweetwater 24
swim (v) 4
swimming (n) 4
swimming
  pool 4
Swiss (cheese)
  70
switch on 12
Switzerland 57
Sydney 7

Irregular verbs

Infinitive form	Past tense	Past participle	Infinitive form	Past tense	Past participle
be	was/were	been	let	let	let
become	became	become	lose	lost	lost
begin	began	begun	make	made	made
break	broke	broken	mean	meant	meant
bring	brought	brought	meet	met	met
build	built	built	pay	paid	paid
buy	bought	bought	put	put	put
catch	caught	caught	read	read	read
choose	chose	chosen	ride	rode	ridden
come	came	come	ring	rang	rung
cost	cost	cost	run	ran	run
cut	cut	cut	say	said	said
do	did	done	see	saw	seen
drink	drank	drunk	sell	sold	sold
drive	drove	driven	send	sent	sent
eat	ate	eaten	shine	shone	shone
fall	fell	fallen	show	showed	shown
feel	felt	felt	shut	shut	shut
fight	fought	fought	sing	sang	sung
find	found	found	sit	sat	sat
fly	flew	flown	sleep	slept	slept
forget	forgot	forgotten	speak	spoke	spoken
freeze	froze	frozen	spend	spent	spent
get	got	gotten	stand	stood	stood
give	gave	given	steal	stole	stolen
go	went	gone	swim	swam	swum
grow	grew	grown	take	took	taken
have	had	had	teach	taught	taught
hear	heard	heard	tear	tore	torn
hide	hid	hidden	tell	told	told
hit	hit	hit	think	thought	thought
hurt	hurt	hurt	throw	threw	thrown
keep	kept	kept	wake	woke	woken
know	knew	known	wear	wore	worn
leave	left	left	win	won	won
lend	lent	lent	write	wrote	written

Listening appendix

Unit 2

1.
A: Directory Assistance. What city?
B: Minneapolis, please.
A: What name?
B: Nelson. Mr. P. 1999 Stinson Boulevard in Columbia Heights.
A: Thank you for calling Minnesota Telephone. The number is 334-9045.

2.
C: Directory Assistance. What city?
D: San Francisco.
C: What name?
D: Slick. Ms. G., at 2400 Fulton Street, San Francisco.
C: Thank you for calling Pacific Bell. The number is 685-0124.

3.
E: Directory Assistance. What city?
F: Miami.
E: What name?
F: Buffett, J., on Alton Road in Miami Beach. I don't know the address.
E: Thank you for calling Southeast Bell. The number is 766-5501.

4.
G: Directory Assistance. What city?
H: Boston, please.
G: What name?
H: Knight, J. It's somewhere in the Jamaica Plain area.
G: There's a J. Knight on Arborway.
H: That's the one.
G: Thank you for calling New England Telephone. The number is 552-7136.

5.
I: Directory Assistance. What city?
J: Chicago.
I: What name?
J: Butterfield. P., on 59th Street, by the Midway airport.
I: Thank you for calling Illinois Bell. The number is 401-0033.

Unit 5

1.
The train from Philadelphia will be five minutes late. The new time of arrival will be 6:50 PM on track three.

2.
The 7:15 PM train from Cincinnati, continuing on to Philadelphia, will now be here at 7:30 PM, arriving on track five. The 7:15 PM train from Cincinnati, continuing on to Philadelphia, will now be here at 7:30 PM on track five.

3.
There will be a one-hour delay on the 7:40 from Chicago and Cleveland. The train will now be here at 8:39 PM, on track four. We apologize for any inconvenience.

4.
The 8:20 arrival from St. Louis will be on track one. This train will be just two minutes late. The St. Louis train will be just two minutes late at 8:22 PM.

Unit 7

This is Channel 35 News. Walter and Betty Busby are recovering tonight in Monterey Hospital. They left Monterey Bay this morning at 6:30 in their boat, *Titanic II*. They were sailing to Australia. Seven miles out of Monterey their engine stopped, and the boat turned over in heavy seas. They held onto the boat, and a helicopter rescued them. This was not Mr. and Mrs. Busby's first accident on the ocean. They have been rescued three times before. They were cold and wet, but cheerful. Mr. Busby said, "We're looking for a bigger boat. We'll get to Australia one day. We had some bad luck."

Unit 14

A: Hello.
B: Good morning. This is the First State Bank. My name's Bridget O'Connor. I'm the manager.
A: Oh, yes?
B: Did you get my letter?
A: What letter was that?
B: Well, I wanted to see you. I called yesterday, but I couldn't get an answer.
A: Was that in the morning?
B: That's right.
A: I'm sorry, I wasn't here. I had to see my doctor. I've had problems with my leg.
B: I wanted to ask you about your account.
A: My account?
B: Yes. You wrote a check for $1,000 last week.
A: $1,000?
B: Yes, and there's only $152.95 in your account.
A: But I don't have an account with First State.
B: Now, look here Mr. Trump…
A: Mr. Trump? Who's Mr. Trump? I'm not Mr. Trump.
B: I'm sorry. Is this 848-3592?
A: Say that again.
B: 848-3592.
A: Ah! This is 848-3952. My name's Sikorski. You have the wrong number.
B: Oh!

Unit 16

5
A: Excuse me, ma'am.
B: Yes?
A: We're doing a traffic survey. Could I ask you a few questions?
B: OK.
A: Your name is?
B: Green. Michelle Green.
A: And…uh…how old are you?
B: 29.
A: Can you drive?
B: Sure.
A: And how long have you been able to drive?
B: Since I was 19.
A: Uh-huh. Where do you live?
B: Oxford Street.
A: Ah, that's not far away. How do you usually get downtown?
B: By bicycle.
A: By bicycle? That's unusual. Thank you.
B: Oh, is that all?
A: Yes, that's it. Thank you very much.

6

A: Excuse me, sir…
C: Yeah? What?
A: May I ask you a few questions?
C: Questions? About what? You're not from the police, are you?
A: No, no. It's just a traffic survey, that's all.
C: Well, all right, then.
A: What's your name?
C: Uh…Jones, Wayne Jones, eh?
A: How old are you, Mr. Jones?
C: Uh…22, eh?
A: Can you drive?
C: Yeah. But I don't drive much.
A: How long have you been able to drive?
C: Mmm…about four years. But I told you, I don't drive much. I come into town on my motorcycle. It's a Harley-Davidson. It's over there. The red one.
A: Mmmm. Where do you live, Mr. Jones?
C: Uh…the university. I'm a student, eh?
A: Oh, really?
C: Yeah. I'm studying philosophy.

Unit 25

Listening 1

1.
Global Airways announces the departure of the 11 o'clock flight GL189 to Houston. This flight is now boarding at Gate Four.

2.
British Airways announces the departure of the 11:30 Concorde service BA001 to London. Would passengers for this flight go immediately to Gate 16.

3.
Would passengers for the 11:25 AeroMexico flight 149 to Mexico City please go immediately to Gate 13, where this flight is now boarding.

4.
This is the last call for Japan Airlines' 10:45 flight 215 to Tokyo. This flight is now closing at Gate 30.

Listening 2

Good morning, ladies and gentlemen. This is your captain speaking. I'd like to welcome you all aboard Global's Flight 179 to Caracas. We're now flying at an altitude of 33,000 feet, and our speed is approximately 500 miles per hour. We'll land in Caracas in three-and-a-half hours at 1:20 local time. The temperature in Caracas is a sunny 87° Fahrenheit; about 31° Celsius. In a few minutes, you'll be able to see the Gulf of Mexico on our left. Our flight attendants will serve lunch in a few minutes. Enjoy your flight, and thank you for choosing Global!

Unit 31

1. I'm from Canada.
2. I've had a lot of English classes.
3. I take a shower every day.
4. I was in class last Sunday.
5. I'm not a millionaire.
6. I've never had a headache.
7. I didn't eat anything yesterday.
8. I don't drive a Cadillac.

Unit 37

Int: First of all, *Animals in Focus.* What did you think of that?
Mrs. Zimmerman: Great. Really great. It was educational, just right for the children. And chimpanzees always amuse me. Much more amusing than Lenny Hill in the next program. Some of his jokes are quite shocking. And young children are watching television at that time of night.
Int: Uh-huh. What about *Texas, Texas?*
Mrs. Zimmerman: The worst kind of TV! This kind of program annoys me. It's all just money and sex. Not interesting.
Int: OK. And the report on violence in the cities? What did you think of that?
Mrs. Zimmerman: A very important program. The problem of violence worries everyone.
Int: The news?
Mrs. Zimmerman: The news always interests me. There isn't enough news on TV.

Int: And lastly, the horror movie.
Mrs. Zimmerman: Well, horror movies like this don't frighten me at all. I just turn them off!

Unit 41

Well, I guess it's difficult to choose just five things out of a whole lifetime. I need a little time to think…. Well, the most important thing for me was the birth of my son, but I guess everyone chooses a birth. But that really changes your life. That's the biggest change, for sure. What else? Strange, I think the assassination of President Kennedy, in 1963. That's a long time ago. Really, a long time. But I was in high school, and for me it's like the line between being a kid and…I don't know, growing up. I don't think it changed *my* life, but I remember it so well. And everything was different after that. So that's two milestones, then. Oh, yes, and the day that I moved into this house. I've lived here for 20 years. I've always loved this house. Then there was my accident. I don't like talking about it, really. I fell down a mountain when I was skiing. I was in the hospital for six weeks. I couldn't walk for nearly a year. What else? That's not all, one more. Let me think, uh, this sounds silly. A few years ago I was in an elevator and it stopped—just like that— between floors. I was alone there for five hours. I was terrified. I thought about my life and my family. I still have nightmares about it.

Unit 44

And finally news about Kimberly Lewis, the athlete from Pennsylvania. Kimberly is jogging across the United States from New York to Los Angeles. She has just arrived in Kansas City, Missouri. Kimberly left New York two months ago, and has traveled nearly 1300 miles. Kimberly has collected nearly

$300,000 for physically challenged children. She has used twelve pairs of running shoes and more than one hundred pairs of socks.

Unit 48

Good morning. I'm Wayne Porter with your latest weather news from Channel 15. Let's look at the national situation first. The Pacific Coast will have clear and sunny skies all day, but it will be quite cold. The Rockies can expect further heavy snowfalls in the north and it will be extremely cold. The Midwest will have strong winds coming down from Canada and these winds will bring a lot of rain into the region. There might be snow in the west of the region later. The Northeast will have cloudy skies with temperatures in the mid-40s. There will be strong winds and heavy rain on the Gulf coast of Texas, and there might be thunderstorms later in the day. These storms might move across into Florida by the early evening. In Florida, it will be a very hot, humid day with cloudy skies, but there won't be any rain in the earlier part of the day. Now let's hear from Joan Zane for more weather news for the Tampa Bay area….

Unit 55

Suzy: Hello.
Adrian: Hi, Suzy. It's me.
Suzy: I'm sorry. Who?
Adrian: It's me, Adrian. Adrian Roth?
Suzy: Oh, hello, Adrian. What's wrong?
Adrian: It's about tonight. I might be late. I'll have to wait until my Dad gets home. He forgot his keys.
Suzy: How late? The movie begins at eight o'clock.
Adrian: Oh, I'll be there before it begins. He'll be home at 7:15. I'll leave as soon as he gets here.
Suzy: What time will you be there?
Adrian: About ten to eight. Is that OK?

Suzy: All right. But I'm not going to stand outside the movie theater all night. Don't be later than eight o'clock, or I won't be there. (Click.)
Adrian: OK. Suzy? Are you still there? Suzy?

Unit 67

"Last night I went to see the new musical at the Lewis and Clark Memorial Theater. It's called *Space Opera* and was written by Tim Webber with music by Andrew Rice. It was a highly entertaining evening and the audience enjoyed every minute of it. The music was performed by the Idaho Symphony Orchestra, and it is really great. The hero is played by soap-opera star Danny Kleen, and he sings most of the best songs. However, the most popular song in the show is 'Starlight Tonight,' and I'm sure it'll be a big hit. It's sung by Lorna Winter, who plays the Queen of Jupiter. Her costumes are sensational. They were designed by Annette Field. One dress cost more than $20,000. There is a CD of the show, available on the Polyglot label, and an illustrated book which is published by Appletree Books. Take my advice—go see it."

Unit 70

Counterperson: Next.
Bob: One Big Greg, one Cheese Greg, one order of fries…
Counterperson: Large or regular?
Bob: Large. And two strawberry shakes.
Counterperson: Is that it?
Bob: Uh-huh. That's all.

Waiter: Hi. I'm Adam and I'm your waiter today. Are you ready to order yet?
Tina: Yes, please. We'd like a plain pizza and a Pizza Palace Special.
Waiter: Would you like regular or large pizzas?
Tina: Both regular, please.
Waiter: Anything to start?

Tina: Yes. A soup and a house salad, please.
Waiter: Sure. It'll take just a couple of minutes.

Counterperson: Hello there, hon. What can I get for you?
Dan: One tuna sandwich and one vegetarian, please.
Counterperson: Will that be white, whole wheat, rye bread, or a roll?
Dan: Whole wheat.
Counterperson: Will there be any drinks with that, hon?
Dan: One coffee, one hot tea.
Counterperson: Is that everything?
Dan: Yeah. That's it.

Unit 78

Manager: I'm sorry but I have to call the police.
Michelle: Oh, no! It's all a terrible mistake! Now I remember! I was talking to my neighbor. His name's David—David Samuels. Anyway, his little boy, Joshua, was with him. You see, Josh was playing with some jars of coffee. He was bored, I guess. David asked him what he was doing. I remember. Then I left them and I did the rest of my shopping. I paid for my groceries and went out into the parking lot. The store detective stopped me there. That's it! Josh put the coffee in my bag. I'm sure that's the answer.
Manager: I'm sorry. I really don't believe you.
(knock on door)
David: Michelle! The cashier told me you were in here. I've just been speaking with Josh. He said that he put a jar in your bag!
Manager: Who are you?
David: I'm Michelle's neighbor. Look, I can explain everything…

Grammar summaries

Unit 4

Present perfect/Past simple

I/You	went	there	yesterday.
He/She	didn't go		last week.
We/They	did not go		in 1986.
			at two o'clock.
			on Monday.

Did	I/you	go	there?
	he/she		
	we/they		

Yes, I did.
No, she didn't.

I	've	gone.
You	have	
We	haven't	
They	have not	
He	's	
She	has	
	hasn't	
	has not	

Have	I	gone?
	you	
	we	
	they	
Has	he	
	she	

Yes, we have.
No, they haven't.

Yes, he has.
No, she hasn't.

Irregular verbs

Present	Past	Perfect
begin	began	begun
dive	dived (or dove)	dived
fall	fell	fallen
go	went	gone
get	got	gotten
hit	hit	hit
hold	held	held
hurt	hurt	hurt
make	made	made
run	ran	run
swim	swam	swum
throw	threw	thrown
win	won	won

Unit 5

Future simple: *to be*

I	'll	be	there	tomorrow.
You	will			next week.
He	won't			next year.
She	will not			next month.
It				next Monday.
We				at two o'clock.
They				later.

Will	I	be	there?
	you		
	he		
	she		
	it		
	we		
	they		

Yes, I will.
No, I won't.

Unit 6

Future simple

I/You	'll	go there.
He/She/It	will	do that.
We/They	won't	see them.
	will not	eat it.

Will	I/you	go there?
	he/she/it	do that?
	we/they	see them?
		eat it?

Yes, he will.
No, we won't.

Unit 8

Review: Past tenses

I	was	sleeping.
He/she		
We/you/they	were	

Was	I	sleeping?	Yes, he was.
	he/she		No, she wasn't.
Were	you/we/they		Yes, you were.
			No, we weren't.

Have	I/you/we/they	ever had a nightmare?	Yes, I have.
Has	he/she		No, he hasn't.

Irregular verbs

Present	Past	Perfect
get up	*got up*	*gotten up*
stand	*stood*	*stood*
sleep	*slept*	*slept*
feed	*fed*	*fed*
meet	*met*	*met*

Unit 9

Requests/Offers

Can I help you?
Could I have a box of throat lozenges, please?
Could you fill this prescription, please?
Should I pay now or later?

Unit 10

Want

I/You We/They	*want* *don't want*	*it.* *them.*
He She	*wants* *doesn't want*	*him.* *her.*

I/You We/They	*want* *don't want*	*to*	*do that.* *see them.*
He She	*wants* *doesn't want*		*meet him.* *talk to her.*

I	*want*	*you*	*to*	*do that.*
You We They	*don't want*	*me* *him* *her* *it*		*see them.* *meet him.* *talk to her.*
He She	*wants* *doesn't want*	*us* *them*		

What Who	*do you want?*
What	*do you want to do?* *do you want her to do?*

Unit 11

Verbs of perception

It	*looks* *feels* *tastes* *sounds* *smells*	*good.*

They	*look* *feel* *taste* *sound* *smell*	*good.*

It looks like a used car.
They feel like fur.
It tastes like an apple.
It sounds like a train.
It smells like coffee.

Unit 12

Irregular verbs

Present	Past	Perfect
fly	*flew*	*flown*
say	*said*	*said*
put	*put*	*put*
understand	*understood*	*understood*
stick	*stuck*	*stuck*

Unit 13

Too/enough

It's too hot for me to drink.
It's cool enough for me to drink.
I'm not strong enough to lift it.
I'm too weak to lift it.

Irregular verbs

Present	Past	Perfect
catch	*caught*	*caught*
forget	*forgot*	*forgotten*
leave	*left*	*left*
bring	*brought*	*brought*

Unit 14

Wanted (to do)/could (do)/had to (do)

I/You He/She We/They	*could* *couldn't* *could not*	*lift it.*

I /You He/She We/They	*had to* *didn't have to* *did not have to*	*carry it.*

I /You He/She We/They	*wanted to* *didn't want to* *did not want to*	*go out.*

Unit 15

Will have to (do)/have had to (do)

I/You He/She We/They	*'ll* *will* *won't* *will not*	*have to*	*wear a uniform.*

Will	*I/you* *he/she* *we/they*	*have to*	*wear a uniform?*

I You We They	*'ve* *have* *haven't* *have never*	*had to*	*wear a uniform.*
He She	*'s* *has* *hasn't* *has never*		

(Unit 15 continued)

Have	I	ever had to wear a uniform?
	you	
	we	
	they	
Has	he	
	she	

Unit 16

Have been able to (do); for; since

I	've	been able to	work	for two days.
You	have			since last Tuesday.
We	haven't			
They	have not			
He	's			
She	has			
	hasn't			
	has not			

Unit 17

Will be able to (do)

I	'll	be able to	go.
You	will		
He	won't		
She	will not		
We			
They			

Will	I	be able to	go?
	you		
	he/she		
	we		
	they		

Yes, I will./No, I won't.
Yes, he will./ No, he won't.

Unit 19

How far/heavy/long/wide/tall (etc.)...?

How	far	is it?
	heavy	are they?
	hot	
	high	
	long	
	old	
	wide	
	deep	

It's/They're	20 miles (away).	(distance)
	20 kilograms.	(weight)
	20° Centigrade.	(temperature)
	20 meters (high).	(height)
	20 meters (long).	(length)
	20 (years old).	(age)
	20 meters (wide).	(width)
	20 meters (deep).	(depth)

Unit 20

Comparison of adverbs

I	drive	slowly.
You	drove	quickly.
We		carefully.
They		carelessly.
		well.
He	drives	badly.
She	drove	fast.

I	drive	more slowly/slower	than	them.
You	drove	more quickly/quicker		us.
We		more carefully		her.
They		more carelessly		him.
		better		
He	drives	worse		you.
She	drove	faster		me.

Unit 21

Irregular verbs

Present	Past	Perfect
bring	brought	brought
mean	meant	meant
ring	rang	rung

Unit 22

Tag questions

It's Howard Smith, isn't it?
You're from New York, aren't you?
You aren't a secretary, are you?
You went to high school, didn't you?
You didn't go to college, did you?

You can speak English, can't you?
You can't speak Arabic, can you?
You've been to Miami, haven't you?
You haven't been to Paris, have you?

Unit 23

Past simple/Past continuous

I	was	working	when	I	heard the news.
He		watching TV		he	saw it on TV.
She				she	
We	were			we	
You				you	
They				they	

It was hard, but I managed to pass.

Unit 25

May I...?

May I see	your passport?
	the contents of your pockets?

Unit 26

Reflexive/emphatic pronouns

I	enjoyed	myself.
You	didn't enjoy	yourself.
He		himself.
She		herself.
We		ourselves.
You		yourselves.
They		themselves.

It	turns	itself	on.
			off.

Unit 27

Comparisons: *as (good) as; as much/many as;* etc.

This (one)	's	as	good	as	that (one).
	is		bad		those (ones).
	isn't		new		
			big		
These (ones)	are				
	aren't				

Juan	has	as	much money	as	Maria.
	doesn't have		many friends		

Juan	speaks	as	well	as	Maria.
	doesn't speak		badly		
			quickly		

Unit 28

Tag questions (continued)

He lives in New York, doesn't he?
She doesn't live in New York, does she?
You believe me, don't you?
You don't like coffee, do you?

You've read that book, haven't you?
He hasn't read it, has he?
She was ill, wasn't she?
She wasn't there, was she?

They weren't there, were they?
We were right, weren't we?
She was driving, wasn't she?
They weren't working, were they?

Unit 29

Socializing

Great to see you!
Let me take your coats.
Go on in.
Help yourself.
I like your dress.
Do you want to dance?
Thanks for coming.
It was nice of you to invite me.
Thanks again.

Unit 30

Reflexives/*each other*

He likes her. She likes him. ....They like each other.
I met you. You met me. ....We met each other.
Marco, you looked at Maria.
Maria, you looked at Marco. ....They looked at each other.

Unit 31

Rejoinders: *So (am) I/Neither (am) I*

	Agreeing	Disagreeing
I'm tired.	So am I.	I'm not.
I've finished.	So have I.	I haven't.
I like cats.	So do I.	I don't.
I was wrong.	So was I.	I wasn't.
I read it.	So did I.	I didn't.
I can swim.	So can I.	I can't.

	Agreeing	Disagreeing
I'm not tired.	Neither am I.	I am.
I haven't finished.	Neither have I.	I have.
I don't like cats.	Neither do I.	I do.
I wasn't wrong.	Neither was I.	I was.
I didn't read it.	Neither did I.	I did.
I can't swim.	Neither can I.	I can.

Unit 32

Prepositions after adjectives

I'm	pleased with	it.
I was	worried about	
You're	good at	
You were	bad at	
	interested in	

I'm	sorry about	him.
I was	sorry for	her.
You're	upset with	them.
You were	rude to	
	tired of	

Unit 33

Confirming; Disagreeing

Yes	No	?
That's right.	That's wrong.	I don't know.
That's correct.	That isn't correct.	I'm not sure.
Of course.	Of course not.	I'm not certain.
That's true.	That isn't true.	
I agree.	I disagree.	

Unit 34

Used to (do)

I	used to	do that.
He	never used to	
We	didn't use to	

Did	they	use to	do that?
	you		
	she		

Unit 35

Indirect commands; indirect statements

| Ask | him | to | go. |
| | | not to | |

| He | asked | him | to | go. |
| | told | | not to | |

He	says	he	can	go.
She	thinks	she	can't	
	knows			
	hopes			
	is sure			

| He | is afraid | he | can't | go. |
| She | is sorry | she | | |

Unit 37

I'm bored/It's boring/It bores me (etc.)

I'm bored.	It's boring.	It bores me.
He's interested.	It's interesting.	It interests him.
She's worried.	It's worrying.	It worries her.
We're shocked.	It's shocking.	It shocks us.
You're annoyed.	It's annoying.	It annoys you.
They're frightened.	It's frightening.	It frightens them.
I'm amused.	It's amusing.	It amuses me.
He's embarrassed.	It's embarrassing.	It embarrasses him.
She's terrified.	It's terrifying.	It terrifies her.
We're excited.	It's exciting.	It excites us.
You're disturbed.	It's disturbing.	It disturbs you.

Unit 38

Should/Shouldn't

I	should	do that.
you	shouldn't	
he	should not	
she		
we		
they		

Should | I | do that?

Yes, you should.
No, you shouldn't.

Unit 39

Defining relative clauses with *that*

It's	the one	that	does that.
He's			
She's			
That's			

| They're | the ones | that | do that. |
| We're | | | |

Unit 40

Present perfect continuous

How long	have	you	been	doing that?
		we		
		they		
	has	he		
		she		
		it		

I	've	been	doing that	for	two years.
You	have				three days.
We				since	1968.
They					Monday.
He	's				
She	has				
It					

Unit 42

Relative clauses (2)

He's the man. I saw him.
She's the woman. He met her.
That's the coat. She was wearing it.
They're the people. We saw them.

He's the man I saw.
She's the woman he met.
That's the coat she was wearing.
They're the people we saw.

Unit 44

Present perfect simple and continuous

| How long | have you | been driving? |
| | has she | |

| I've | been driving | for two hours. |
| She's | | |

| How | much | have you | done? |
| | many | has she | |

How far | have you | driven?

Unit 45

Relative clauses (3)

She's the woman. I met her. ....She's the woman I met.
She's the woman. She met me. ..She's the woman that met me.

Unit 47

-ing forms: like/afraid of/interested in

| I | like | reading. |
| | don't like | swimming. |

I'm	afraid of	doing that.
	tired of	
	interested in	

Do you like reading?

Unit 48

Probability: will/might/won't

It may rain.

| We | might | go to Pennsylvania. |
| | might not | |

What will the weather be like in Texas?

| …during | the morning/the afternoon/ |
| | the evening/ the night. |

Unit 49

Quantity: plenty of/enough/too (much)

There's	a little	gravy.
	enough	
	plenty of	
	a lot of/lots of	
	too much	

There are	a few	potatoes.
	enough	
	plenty of	
	a lot of/lots of	
	too many	

Start /Begin doing

| Start | doing something. |
| Begin | |

He's getting upset.

Unit 50

Prepositions of place/movement

Is this the way to the station?
Can you tell me the best route to the station?
Does this bus go to Fiftieth Street?
I'm looking for the station.
I'm trying to find the station.
Can you direct me to the station?

Directions/location

Turn left/right.
Take the first/second street on the left/right.
Go straight ahead.
Cross the bridge.
Go under the bridge.
Continue to ….

Unit 51

Indirect questions

Ask him if he's married.   Are you married?
Ask her where she lives.   Where do you live?

Unit 52

Indirect questions (continued)

Do you know	what it is?
Do you have any idea	why he did it?
	if he works here?

I don't know	what it is.
I have no idea	why he did it.
I wonder	if he works there.

Unit 53

Review: relative clauses

Small boats are carrying detergent. They are working around the slick.
Small boats, **which are carrying detergent,** are working around the slick.

Unit 54

Nobody/Nothing/Nowhere else

The street was empty
except for Sara Garcia..........................There was nobody else.
The room was empty
except for a chair...............................There was nothing else.
All the hotels were closed,
except for one. ....There was nowhere else.

Unit 55

Future + when/before/after/as soon as/until

I	'll	leave	when	she comes.
	will		before	
			after	
			as soon as	

| I | won't | leave | before | she comes. |
| | will not | | until | |

We | 'll | wait | until | she comes.

Unit 56

Conditional (type 1)

I	'll	do this	if	you	do	that.
	will				don't do	
	won't				do not do	
	will not					

Unit 59

Letter format

Beginnings	Endings
Dear Sir: Dear Madam: Dear Sir or Madam:	Yours sincerely, Yours truly,
Dear Mr. Smith: Dear Mrs. Smith: Dear Miss Smith: Dear Ms. Smith:	Yours sincerely, Sincerely yours,
Dear John, Dear Mary,	Sincerely, Best wishes,

Useful expressions

I'd like to…
I wish to…
I'd be grateful if you could…
Could you please…
Thanking you in anticipation.

If you want to send money by mail, write:
I enclose a check/money order for ($30).

Unit 60

Past perfect (continued)

| I/You
He/She
We/They | 'd
had
hadn't
had not | seen | it. |

| Had | I/you
he/she
we/they | seen | it? |

Yes, I had.
No, I hadn't.

Unit 61

Past perfect (continued)

It happened <u>when</u> I had just finished college.
<u>When</u> I arrived, they had gone into class.
<u>As soon as</u> I had parked the car, I rushed back to the bank.

Unit 62

Past perfect continuous

| I/You
He/She
We/They | 'd
had
hadn't
had not | been reading | for

since | a long time.
two hours.

six o'clock.
Monday. |

| How long | had | he | been | reading? |

(Unit 62 Continued)

Reflexives

I did it myself.
Do it yourself!
He saw it himself.
She's seen it herself.

We made it ourselves.
You did it yourselves.
They'd seen it themselves.

Unit 63

Made of

| It's
They're | made of | gold. |

Unit 64

Passive: present and past simple

It	is was	made in produced in imported from exported to	the U.S.
They	are were		

| It | was | invented
discovered
written
made | by | her. |

Unit 65

Passive (continued)

| It | is
was
has been
will be | done. |

| Is
Was | it | done? |

| Has
Will | it | been
be | done? |

Unit 66

Passive (extension)

It	is	being	done.
They	are		
It	had	been	
They			

Someone did that. … It was done.
Someone does that. … It is done.
Someone is doing that. … It is being done.
Someone has done that. … It has been done.
Someone had done that. … It had been done.
Someone will do that. … It will be done.

Unit 67

Passive: extension with *can be*

It | can be | done.

Unit 68

Become

He became popular.
She became his wife.

Relative clauses (continued)

He went to Hollywood. He made several movies there.
He went to Hollywood where he made several movies.

Unit 69

Conditionals (types 1 and 2)

If	I	had enough money	I	'd	buy a car.
		could drive		would	
		were rich			

What	would	you	do	if	you	had	enough money?
						were	rich?

Unit 70

Giving advice (*If I were you…*)

I'd have the special if I were you.   or   *If I were you, I'd have the special.*

I wouldn't have a large one if I were you.   or   *If I were you, I wouldn't have a large one.*

Unit 71

Conditional (type 2)

If	I	were Governor,	I	'd	spend money
		could choose,		would	on highways.
				wouldn't	
				would not	

Would you spend money on highways?
Yes, I would/No, I wouldn't.

Unit 73

Passive with modals

Someone	will	do it.
	must	
	can	
	might	
	could	
	should	

It	will	be done.
	must	
	can	
	might	
	could	
	should	

No one	will	do that.
	must	
	can	
	could	
	should	

It	won't	be done.
	mustn't	
	can't	
	couldn't	
	shouldn't	
	might not	

Unit 74

Reported speech: basic tenses

Direct speech	Indirect speech
Maria said, "This is my bag."	*Maria said that was her bag.*
Maria said, "These aren't my pens."	*Maria said those weren't her pens.*
Kevin said, "I like tea."	*Kevin said he liked tea.*
Kevin said, "I don't like coffee."	*Kevin said he didn't like coffee.*
Anne said, "I can dance well."	*Anne said she could dance well.*
Anne said, " I can't cook."	*Anne said she couldn't cook.*
Paul said, "I have a new apartment."	*Paul said he had a new apartment.*
Paul said, "My wife doesn't have a car."	*Paul said his wife didn't have a car.*
Maria said, "I've been to France."	*Maria said she'd been to France.*
Maria said, "My mother hasn't been there."	*Maria said her mother hadn't been there.*
Carlos said, "I bought it last week."	*Carlos said he had bought it the week before.*
Carlos said, "I didn't buy it yesterday."	*Carlos said he hadn't bought it the day before.*
Jean said, "I'll do it tomorrow."	*Jean said she would do it the next day.*
Jean said, "I won't do it next week."	*Jean said she wouldn't do it the following week.*

this	becomes	*that*
these		*those*
here		*there*
now		*then*
today		*that day*
yesterday		*the day before*
tomorrow		*the next day*
this week		*that week*
last month		*the month before*
next year		*the following year*

Unit 75

Reported speech: questions

Direct question

What's your name?
Are you a secret agent?

Reported question

She asked me	*what my name was.*
	if I was a secret agent.

Unit 76

Reported speech (extension)

Direct speech	Reported speech
could	*could*
should	*should*
might	*might*

Unit 77

To (have/get) something done

I'm going to have	*my car tuned up.*
I've just had	*my suit cleaned.*
I had	*my shoes fixed.*
I should have	*my coat lengthened.*

Unit 80

Future plans

What	*are you going*	*to do?*
	are you planning	
	would you like	
	do you want	
	do you intend	
	do you hope	